THE SANDBOX

THE SANDBOX
Stories of Human Spirit and War

Foreword by Paul Rieckhoff

Mike Liguori

Grizzly Peak Press
Kensington, California

For information contact:

Grizzly Peak Press
350 Berkeley Park Boulevard
Kensington, California 94707
grizzlypeakpress.com

The Sandbox is published by Daniel N. David
and is distributed by Grizzly Peak Press.

Front cover photo courtesy of the author

Note: *The story "Smokes" was witnessed by me. To protect the privacy of my fellow marines, I wrote the story in the first person to give the reader an inside perspective.*

Design, layout and typesetting by
Liquid Pictures
www.liquidpictures.com

ISBN Number: 978-0-9839264-2-9
Library of Congress Number: 2012943925

Printed in the United States of America

Contents

This book is dedicated to my family, my friends, and everyone I served with. I will never forget the love, compassion and loyalty all of you have shown me during this journey. God Bless you all.

Acknowledgments

Helen Kao Chang, Editor
Professor Frances Turner
Professor Marilyn Thomas
Professor Craig Medlen
Professor Lowell Pratt
Aunt Camille
Menlo College Staff and Faculty
for their undying support

The love of my life, Sabrina

United States Marine Corps
Iraq and Afghanistan Veterans of America

Last but not least,
all of you who told me to never
stop writing and to follow my dreams...

Foreword

THE HARD ROAD BACK

TEN YEARS. TWO WARS. THOUSANDS
killed. Thousands more wounded. Trillions
spent. One half of one percent of Americans who served.

That's the legacy of the wars of Iraq and Afghanistan. By
the numbers, at least. The real legacy lies in the stories. Stories
of battle. Stories of heroism. Stories of fallen comrades, stories of
long, sleepless patrols, stories of dust storms and mountain paths
and smells that can't ever be totally described, only remembered.

But then comes the journey home, which is a story unto itself.

Ever since returning from Iraq in 2004, it's become
quite clear to me that many Americans want to hear about
the war stories from over there — but aren't too interested
in the war stories of back here. It doesn't work like that,
though. Not for the men and women who fight on our behalf.

In many ways, the war on the homefront is longer and
messier than the one fought overseas. And in this era of an all-
volunteer force, it is too often one fought alone — something
that is having a tragic and terrifying effect on our new veterans' community. In 2011, it was estimated that more Iraq and

Afghanistan veterans committed suicide than actually perished in combat, an unfathomable reality that we're all to blame for.

You want a war story? Mike Liguori's The Sandbox has plenty of that, chronicling his two deployments to Iraq as a United States Marine. His writing is sharp and hard-hitting, and has that rare ability of putting the reader in the moment.

More than finding out what it was like "over there" though, The Sandbox offers readers a real and sobering gut check of what it's like for vets "back here." Mike bravely shares his experiences transitioning from combat to campus. Though he initially felt out of sync with his civilian peers and struggled a bit with pills prescriptions from the VA, he persevered and graduated in 2011 with a Bachelors degree in Business Management. He is the founder of a nonprofit that helps veterans develop professional careers and landed a beat with Examiner.com as a Veterans Affairs correspondent.

He is a success story for this New Greatest Generation. But it wasn't an easy road there, as you'll see in the pages that follow.

He earned it the hard way.

-- Paul Rieckhoff, author of
Chasing Ghosts: Failures and Facades in Iraq: A Soldier's Perspective,
Executive Director of Iraq and Afganistan Veterans of America.

THE SANDBOX

The Beginning

KUWAIT

MOST OF OUR UNIT SAT SILENT FOR THE duration of the trip to the Middle East. It was tempting for someone to cause a scene on the airplane just so nobody had to think about what the hell they had gotten themselves into. It had been three years since the World Trade Center burned at the hands of terrorists. Most of us were seniors in high school at the time. I remember as a senior sitting in chemistry class, watching the towers fall violently to the ground. Smoke covered the city blocks of New York like a blanket. It was disturbing hearing the broadcaster on the news tell about reports of bodies falling from the forty-fourth floor. Never in my life had I been so hurt and angry at the same time.

We left Frankfurt, Germany, hours away from our destination to Kuwait City. I spent the whole entire flight over from California sitting, legs crossed with my gear tucked in between my knees, waiting for my chance to fight and kill the enemy. You could tell the guys who had been to the Middle East before. They were ones chewing gum with their eyes closed, headphones on, books folded open in their laps. They had driven through miles of terrain from Kuwait to Baghdad during the initial invasion in 2003. They kicked their feet up without a care in the world for where they were going. Going to Iraq was another day at the office.

The guys like me, who had no idea what the Middle East had in store, couldn't sleep a wink. I've never been that quiet in my whole life as I sat in my aisle seat. I couldn't stop staring down at the digital print on my uniform. My hands had a slight tremble to them. Even though I was tired, I couldn't close my eyes. Iraq was just too close for me to think about anything else. I couldn't deter my mind to think about anything peaceful or calm. Iraq and the uncertainty of war kept me alert and anxious. The door was going to open any minute now. The weather was about to be hot as hell with nothing but sand beneath my feet.

All I ever heard about Iraq were stories told to me from those who were in the 2003 invasion. The stories were filled with unexplainable acts and hectic events filled with comedy. Back at my previous duty station in Okinawa, a corporal told me he once was driving down this road, with three others in an unarmored Humvee only their rifles pointed out the windows. A Rocket Propelled Grenade (RPG) had been shot directly at them by insurgents, slicing the air with more and more speed. It gained ground faster as the corporal frantically looked for a way to avoid it. It moved at such an alarming rate, the four men in the Humvee could think of nothing but their own death, how their faces were to be burned to a crisp and their bodies shipped home in a casket.

Right when the RPG was to strike the Humvee, it hit the front grill, smoking and whistling until it stopped abruptly. The corporal couldn't believe what he saw. Frozen and shocked, the corporal and the three others drove the rest of the way to Al Nasiriyah, RPG still in the front grill, saved by the grace of God. After he finished his story, his eyes filled with small tears as he lit a cigarette and walked back into his corner office at the motor pool.

Other stories involved Marines pushing through the kill zones of every town they had come across in Iraq while they drank bottles of Canadian whiskey. The more violence they saw, the more bloodshed they had witnessed, the more bottles they polished off at the end of the night. The constant shots from rifles, explosions of grenades and dead bodies were too much at times. Marines of the invasion told me the only way to keep motivated to continue fighting was nightly consumption of whiskey. When night was upon them, they drank close to one another underneath the desert moon until they passed out, waking up the next day to see it all again.

Despite all the violence I anticipated upon my arrival from these stories, there was a story or two filled with comedy that somewhat eased my anxious anticipation of the Middle East. A close friend of mine, Brock, said that during the initial push into Iraq, he was in the middle of showering. Brock always had to look good. It didn't matter if he was going to be digging ditches or taking out the trash, Brock had to look presentable at all times. His head had to be shaved bald. His face had to be smooth as ever. Even his uniform had to be pressed even though the new uniforms the Marines issued to us could be thrown in the dryer and minutes later worn as if it had been pressed. When Brock decided to shower at the border of Kuwait and Iraq, it wasn't showering as most of you would picture -a tub with streaming hot water shooting from a silver shower head. It was a shower where my naked friend had his gunner pour water onto him as Brock attempted to get one last shower in before his unit went to Iraq. In the middle of scrubbing himself clean as quick as he could, his convoy decided to leave earlier than intended. The trucks fired up, everyone in his unit climbed into their trucks ready to leave as Brock, naked and surprised, looked for his pants as fast as he could, hoping not to be left behind.

We touched down in Kuwait City hours later as I felt my uneasiness rise. The plane door finally opened in Kuwait City as an intense heat wave infiltrated the cabin. It was overpowering as the air went from a cool, tolerable breeze to suffocating, sweltering heat. I grabbed my gear quickly from between my knees and from the top compartment of the cabin and pushed towards the front exit of the plane. The closer I got to the door, the more the heat began to take effect. Every small step made my gear feel twice as heavy. As I exited the plane, a flash of white light hit my face-the sun beating down on me. I felt beads of sweat immediately fall down my face and running down the bridge of my nose. When I had a chance to look up enough just to see the landscape, Kuwait was everything I thought the Middle East was, miles of sand with splashes of green bushes.

I walked fast down the airplane stairs, bags held in my hands with a firm grip. I headed towards the small bus waiting on the runway. As the bus filled up, the stereo played "99 Problems" by Jay-Z, which made things a little more comforting. I never knew how widespread hip-hop was until I heard it on that bus in Kuwait. It was funny as hell to hear American hip-hop in the Middle East. It reminded me of a more modern version of the Vietnam War where "Run through the Jungle" by Credence Clearwater Revival was playing in the background of the deep jungle. It was the Vietnam War soundtrack; a song filled with lyrics of gunfire, nightmares and never looking back again against the patriotic rhythms of electric guitars and drums. The Iraq War soundtrack consisted of song about shooting at the police, money, and not giving a fuck about critics. It consisted of deep bass lines along with lyrics that made me want to nod my head in rhythm. It may not have been as appropriate as music with anti-war lyrics, but hearing Jay-Z made me feel comfortable. It made feel that I had a piece of America with me.

The bus started up and we started to move toward our next destination: Camp Victory. The terrain looked the same all around. I wish I could see one beach filled with girls in bikinis, just like the view sweet California had given me. The boredom of small mounds of sand and small cars driving with reckless abandon bothered me. The roads were poorly paved, potholes sprinkled through each lane. I leaned my head on the glass, feeling the windowpane holding me up as I attempted to get some rest.

Just as I closed my eyes, the bus ran over a pothole that shook me. I opened my eyes to the chipped, red painted wood entrance sign of Camp Victory that featured an eroded American flag. The gates had lifted and we drove slowly past the sign, rocking back and forth across the sandy terrain until we were inside on the camp's roads. There were no paved roads in Camp Victory, only gravel roads with small ditches spread throughout. The camp was built into small square blocks like a metropolitan city. Large circus-like tents stood on each of the blocks, housing hundreds of military personnel awaiting their departure into Iraq or waiting for their flight home to the U.S. The bus stopped alongside a metal building that had tin roofing and a couple of windows by the door. It looked like a bigger version of a solitary confinement unit at a prison. We all stepped off, making sure sunglasses were on and our sea bags in hand. The sun was scorching; heat had never been so hot on the back of my neck. I was sweating just standing in place.

Once I took that first step onto the ground of Camp Victory, going to fight in a war became real. All the training, the endless amounts of physical training I had done amounted to this moment of stepping onto foreign soil. I felt the earth beneath my boots. I felt my rifle slung over my back. My pants had a couple layers of sand around the ankles. I couldn't leave; no getting back on the bus and trying to make my way back to Kuwait City Airport and hopefully catch a flight home. There was no way out and I was fine with that.

The gear strapped to our bodies, banged against our legs, making small notes and beats matching the pattern of our steps. Like ants marching, we lined up, filing inside a shelter and shuffling over plywood boards covering every square inch of the sandy floor. Inside, the cots were worn down, some burned with cigarette holes. The cots and the building weren't much but it was hell of a lot better than being outside in the sweltering heat.

Staff Sergeant stood in the middle of the shelter, hands on his hips as he addressed us.

"All right marines, listen up. Our flight into Iraq is heading out at 2000 tonight. So don't get too comfortable. Just rest, grab some chow and be prepared to hit the ground running. Good to go?"

We all replied with fake motivation, "Oorah, Staff Sergeant!" I looked across the squad bay as Staff Sergeant walked out of the building into the desert sun. No one was excited to be here, especially after the twenty-one hour flight from California. But the reason most of us were here was to go to war. We were here to fight for all those back home. I was here to seek revenge on those who bombed the U.S. I was also here to prove to myself that I could go to war. I had never done anything challenging before joining the Marines. War would verify that I was tough, that I was a real bad ass.

Staff Sergeant was one of those guys that had watched the movie <u>Roadhouse</u> one too many times, thought he could walk around and kick everyone's ass. He tried to be cool and calm like Patrick Swayze but ended up being bombastic and erratic like the villain. He was on the shorter side of stature even though his physique resembled Hercules. I always thought he took steroids or some form of performance enhancing drugs since his face was chiseled with veins that popped out with every word he uttered in that asshole tone of his.

He was a former drill instructor, tough as nails but that was his downfall. He was just tough and never showed you a side that allowed you to connect with him. I never got a chance to know who he was outside of the uniform. He always hid behind his rank, never letting me know his first name or where he was from. All I knew in the weeks prior to this deployment was that he was the type of Marine I wanted to be with when combat started. He would gather our platoon at the motor pool back on Camp Pendleton and talk to us about combat, his experiences in Mogadishu, Somalia and what he felt when he got shot at. He talked about his laughter as rockets and rounds flew above him in the back of a five-ton truck. It was his way of dealing with the fear of death. He said that laughter made everything easier. It made the enemy feel like they were a bunch of pussies and they had fucked with the wrong guys. That was the same attitude Staff Sergeant told us we had to take into combat.

I admired him because he loved the Marines so much, but it was like he wasn't human. It was like he was just programmed to serve in war and the Marines. There was no room for compassion or empathy in his combat-hardened body. Being out in the desert with us made it hard for him to show any emotion. He was the hard-charging platoon sergeant we needed if there was a firefight. If he showed us that he had a sensitive side, most of us would have seen his high motivation and war stories as part of a façade to cover his fear. It wasn't part of his genetic code to be compassionate and fight. He had a job of bringing us back home alive. Fighting in combat, laughing at his enemy was the only way he knew how to be.

Waiting for our flight to Iraq heightened the anxiety in the room. The silence was deafening. We were all fatigued from the long journey, but knowing that hours from now we would be in a combat zone made us all uneasy. It was the one time that I will never forget where everyone looked at everyone else and didn't say a single word. The comforts of our everyday lives in America were nonexistent. There was no warm pillow or blanket to come home to. It was me and my platoon. We were going to shoot people who we didn't know.

I sat on my cot, disassembling my rifle to lubricate and clean the inside. I glanced occasionally throughout the weapon cleaning at the others cleaning their weapons. We all possessed the ability to end a man's life and didn't have to feel apologetic for it. We didn't have to know who the terrorists were nor did we care to know them. All we had to do was pull the trigger. It sounded too easy if you asked me.

I couldn't sleep before the flight into Iraq. There was too much going on in my mind for me to be relaxed and sleep. I couldn't help but wonder what was going to become of me in this war. I wanted to show myself how courageous I was. I wanted some sort of medal so I could show how brave I was to anyone that I met. Even if it meant dying in war, I just wanted my name to be that of being a hero. I wanted to be remembered as one.

It was nice to think about my own personal contributions, how one firefight could make me a war hero or a fallen hero. I think everyone that sits and awaits war thinks about what would come of them, how the next months would be filled with unknown events, endless danger, and ordinary terrain. But my personal quest to be a legend was never the motivation behind signing up for the Marines. I signed up for this moment sitting on my cot, cleaning my weapon. I signed up for revenge.

Human Spirit and War

KIDS

Nov. 2004 Operation Iraqi Freedom II Tour I

"*I STILL HAVEN'T SEEN COMBAT. I STILL haven't seen what I had imagined it to be, rounds coming at you with hand-to-hand fighting in the trenches against the enemy. A couple months out here, I have nothing to tell my friends and family back home. I thought war was going to be constant battle. I thought it was going to be days filled with grenades and firefights. I just have been driving miles and miles without a single firefight to show for it. It is a little discouraging that I haven't had a chance to kill. All those hours I spent cleaning weapons seem pointless. I keep getting this itch to shoot anything while I'm out on the roads. I just want to kill something. I want to tell my friends I killed out here, that it was one less terrorist they had to worry about.*

All the days I spent out in the field at Camp Pendleton simulating combat, clearing houses in four man squads feels like it was for nothing. Even though major combat operations ended months earlier, there is still a massive amount of chaos and no centralized government. More people are dying around the Sunni

Triangle and the units on base with us are taking more fire every time they leave the confines of Al Asad Air Base. Even the mortar attacks on base have increased. I suppose I could tell everyone back home that I had seen plenty of bombs and Improvised Explosive Devices (IED) during my convoy runs. Maybe everyone back home would find that to be compelling.

The mental toll of the convoys has grown immensely. The monotony of them, the prolonged security halts, and the regular trips to Al Quim are wearing on me. The kids of the village are the biggest threat that we have had. It is hard to understand why they would throw rocks and scream at us as we drive through their town since none of the kids are probably older than eleven. What did they know about hatred or picking a fight?

Guys in my platoon get pissed off and retaliate back with a mix of profanity and rocks. I try hard not to join the retaliation but I end up participating sometimes by throwing rocks. It is hard not to. They are only kids but I don't want to be looked at by the others as if I am I scared or not part of our unit. I try to be peaceful with the kids despite the difficulty of reining in my aggression. Most of the time, I would try to offer peace by giving food or candy to them or a simple wave of my hand.

I hope the kids will remember me for my acts of kindness and that I wasn't hostile toward them so that when I come up to Al Quim again, I come through safely. But no matter what we did as a unit or I do individually, all the kids knew was that we were Americans and that was enough for them to hate us."

I woke up every morning to the same distant alarm at 5:00 a.m. followed by my rack mate's ass hanging through the missing bar of the top bunk. Waking up to his ass in my face every morning the past months was starting to get old. The alarm was getting old too. It was some other guy's alarm on the other side of the room and its constant nagging sounded like cats howling. I kept my running shoes close by so that when the alarm started to shriek, I could shut it off with a quick flick of my wrist. Just five minutes of uninterrupted sleep without looking up at another guy's ass or hearing the alarm scream would have been nice.

Once other guys started moving, I would force myself to get up and prepare for the long convoy ahead. I usually packed my bag with the same stuff: Red Bull, cans of smokeless tobacco, and my iPod. I would put on the same camouflage utilities that I had worn for the past two weeks and the sweat-stained green shirt that I'd worn for the past four days. I tried to get out of the barracks as fast I could while it was still dark outside. Staff Sergeant would hold platoon shave checks early in the morning to make sure we looked like Marines, clean-cut and ready for war. He would tell us that just because we were in a combat zone didn't mean we had to look like a bag of ass. I was trying to stay alive and vigilant on the road, focused, instead of worrying about if my face was clean shaven.

I arrived at the motor pool just as the sun broke its head over the horizon and walked directly to my truck parked away from the entrance. It was quiet each morning and the air was crisp before the heat of the desert made its appearance. It was also the time when I got to pretend I wasn't in Iraq. I would hide behind my truck; take some breaths in as I pulled a serving of tobacco from my can and inserted it into my lower lip. I leaned against the passenger door and thought about being on a beach somewhere. I thought about how nice it was sitting on that beach with cold beers, nothing but the waves crashing on the sandy beach. It was paradise. It was my time in the morning to remove myself from this place. It never lasted longer than a couple of minutes before the others trickled in to the motor pool. But I enjoyed the few minutes against my truck where my fears and anxiety would disappear into the ocean of my beach.

The others would bang gear around, start to bring over the machine guns to be mounted on top of the trucks. There were others who dug into the Meal Ready to Eat (MRE) boxes looking for hand wipes to wipe their asses with in case they had to shit out on the road. Baby wipes were like gold in Iraq. No one wanted to wipe themself with toilet paper because it was 100-plus degrees and the sweat would make the toilet paper stick to your ass. The port-a-johns would usually start to fill up as guys would complain about the food from the chow hall because it made their stomachs turn after they had eaten there. Most of the time, a few guys hadn't had an opportunity to go to the bathroom before we departed. They had to go out on the road. That was the last thing you wanted, to have to pop a squat between the trucks, your pants around your ankles, and then all of a sudden, find yourself in the midst of a firefight or an IED ambush.

The convoy briefs on any given day were pretty much the same. The convoy commander and assistant convoy commander would call for us to gather in a formation to pass information about the roads or something extremely important had happened within the last 24 hours, like a change in insurgent activity or a road closed and an alternate route needed to be taken. But it ended being the same information, presented in the same way, each convoy. "We're going to this base, the roads are dangerous, watch out for IEDs, and we have no air support." After a month full of repetitive convoy briefs, I never took any of the information seriously. I didn't bother to pay attention to the hazards of the road but rather think about when I was going to get a chance to kill. Thoughts of killing and death were always on my mind when I went on convoys. No matter that I tried to think of something happy or pretend I was on the beach, the thoughts of my rifle piercing the chest of an insurgent overrode all the others.

Our unit was headed to Al Quim today and our platoon commander, Lieutenant Blondie, wasn't going with us. She decided to let her peer, This Lieutenant, be the convoy commander. This Lieutenant's convoy experience was apparent in her lack of ability to disseminate information. She was stumbling over her words, fumbling with papers in her hands, not knowing what information needed to be said or how the briefs went. Of course, no one laughed at her inability to communicate or her obviously limited experience commanding convoys. It wasn't a laughing matter. Guys in the back of the brief were whispering how fucked we were, how shitty it was that Lieutenant Blondie would take her day off on the day we were going to Al Quim. I was afraid more of This Lieutenant than I was of an IED or a firefight.

When the formation was dismissed, I just walked away. No response of "Oorah" or "Yes, Ma'am," as I usually did after the briefs, just walked away with my head down. My mind raced with thoughts of how the port-a- johns looked more and more appealing for me to hide out in so that I wouldn't have to put my life on the line. Despite my fears, I jumped into the cab of the truck hoping that the convoy would move fast as possible so that I could come back to Al Asad and enjoy the little amount of safety I had in Iraq.

The gunner above me was a real nice guy, reminded me a lot of an accountant disguised as a lethal weapon. He was very articulate, graduated from college and was doing the whole reserve thing for the love of the Marines. In spite of his love for the brotherhood and the camaraderie the Marines offered, he had times, just like me, when he hated the monotonous bullshit. His dislike usually showed through his quips and smart-ass remarks. His jokes were usually funny, but what made them hilarious was that he would laugh immediately after he told one. Even if he said something that wasn't particularly funny, I had to laugh once he did. During our security halts, he would light up a Marlboro Red and shout down to me jokes or thoughts he had about Iraq, like the time when he told me how the Marine Corps should take him out to dinner, or at least ask him his name before they tried to screw him again and send him out to Iraq again for a 2nd deployment. Though I was dreading this convoy especially, his humor made light of being out here. It made me want to keep driving.

Hours later, we were passing through the village of Al Quim, where the infamous kids were ready to pop out of their houses and come toward our direction. They were notorious for their erratic response to our presence, throwing rocks at us one moment and then waving at us, clapping as if we were heroes. It was hard trying to greet them with open arms like you usually would with kids. With these kids, you never knew what to expect, they were so volatile. I started to scan each kid quick, making sure they had no weapons on them. I noticed one kid in particular, he was playing soccer with his friends, laughing and even trying to steal a piece of candy from one of the others that had been thrown by one of our guys. The kid was trying to peel his friend's fingers back to grab it, but the closer he got, the more furiously his friend would try to shake him off eventually pushing the kid to the ground. As I kept my eyes on him, the kid glanced at me, slowly picked himself off the ground as he dusted his shirt off. With a look of disdain, he raised one hand into the shape of a small handgun, and pointed it directly at me. He pulled the imaginary trigger with his index finger, smirking as if he had hit me with a pretend bullet while I exited the village.

We pulled into the base minutes later. The base of Al Quim, building painted in shades of green and gray used to be an old loading station for freight trains just outside the village. There were holes on the sides of the buildings with rust complementing the roofs. There were only two to three major buildings, with a smattering of small shacks made out of plywood next to them. The whole camp was no bigger than a small football stadium. The borders on the base were lined with barb wire and sand bunkers eight feet tall. It was an open camp with very little protection from sniper rounds or incoming enemy mortars. Usually, whenever we came into a base, I felt safer than I did when I was on the road. Bases such as Al Asad made us feel safer since they were so big and the units were spread out across it. There was always some sort of staging area away from the fence line so insurgents couldn't take shots at us. But places like Al Quim, where small shacks made out of plywood, buildings with rusted metal roofing and a staging area right by the entrance with no concealment made me question how safe I really was.

This Lieutenant directed each of us to go into different parts of the camp to off-load the supplies. I hadn't eaten in a while and I decided to dig into the MRE box wedged into the small opening between the cab and the truck bed while our truck was being offloaded. MREs were some of the worse tasting food I ever ate. The crackers tasted like cardboard. Most of the meals didn't sound that pleasant. The mini water heater inside the MRE barely heated up the food. Whenever I didn't find an entire meal that was appealing or worth trying to digest, I would scavenge for a meal that had peanut butter or jalapeno cheese inside, and try to use them to barter. Peanut butter and jalapeno cheese were as valuable as jewels and made most meals quite delicious. Guys would even open and look in other MRE bags, hoping to score one of the two. They would mix and match the ingredients, creating their own signature dishes; it was like being on an episode of *Iron Chef.* Lucky for me, I had found jalapeno cheese spread and was able to find crackers as well. I made a sandwich since nothing else looked too appealing. I sat on the hood of my truck, scanning the surroundings of the base as the sun made its way towards the horizon.

As I was eating, I couldn't help but notice the tired, exhausted Marines stationed here. They all walked, kicking stones or dirt as their heads were slouched towards the ground. They seemed miserable. The amenities we had at Al Asad were stellar in comparison to what Al Quim offered these Marines. I wished they had access to what I had at Al Asad. Their chow hall was subpar and the computer café only had two computers working at a time with very slow internet access. Plus, they dealt with violence on a daily basis, like when an Al Quim Marine during the off-load told me to wear my helmet on base due to a sniper shooting at the entrance of the camp a couple days prior. Two Marines entered the base not wearing their helmets and the sniper was able to kill them both.

When those Marines were killed, the guy told us he knew them. He had chow with them regularly. They were part of the same unit. They had a lot in common. I heard the sadness and grief in his voice as he told me about the incident. He was trying hard to hold back the tears behind his eyes. While he walked away towards the cluster of buildings, I couldn't help but to think about how close I was to being a story. Our unit had our share of violence involving bombs and mortar attacks but the Marines of Al Quim's violence involved mortar attacks, roadside bombs, and the loss of two friends who weren't wearing their helmets.

The desert sun descended behind the horizon as the dark midnight sky immediately came on like a planetarium show. I was about to call it a night since our supplies had been off-loaded and it was getting close to 1900. Only half of the other trucks were in the staging lot with me and our battalion had instituted a rule that no unit could leave any base after 1900 due to the increase of violence happening at night around the province.

I started to unroll my sleeping bag and stuff a pillow case with t-shirts to rest my head. Right as I was settling into the sleeping bag, This Lieutenant decided to pass the word that we were going to head back to Al Asad regardless if we were approaching 1900. Everyone in the convoy was relaying the message to one another, giving each other knowing and tragic looks as if their dog had died. This Lieutenant's decision didn't settle with me; my stomach was being tied in knots. The journey ahead felt ominous. There was something wrong with this decision. There was something wrong with that little boy shooting his hand at me from earlier. It just felt dark.

Trucks started to pull into the staging lot as time went by while I rolled my sleeping bag back up, cursing under my breath about leaving Al Quim at night. My hope was that Battalion Headquarters would say "no" to her request to head back due to the time but they cleared her for travel back to Al Asad. I felt fearful. I felt nervous of the unknown that loomed in the village but the Marine side of me brought thoughts of rounds lightly accented by trails of green, heading towards me and returning fire with my rifle, grimacing with every ounce of aggression to deflect the ambush. A firefight would give me the credibility I needed to say I was combat-hardened. My friends would be in awe of my combat experience. They would praise my courage. I would be able to tell them about being shot at, returning fire, and surviving. Men in the shit, bullets flying by me, war faces in a full, fledged rage. A true war story told from my point of view. I might get to see my first action tonight, my first real shot at combat. Maybe leaving wouldn't be so bad at all.

We gathered in formation as This Lieutenant started to go over convoy protocol. The more she spoke about tonight's ride home, the idea of seeing combat and becoming glorified by my friends grew on the forefront of my mind. A wave of doubt battled my want to see action and fight. She mentioned we would be bringing Iraqi civilians with us and escorting them back to Al Asad. We had to protect them as if they were Americans, but I had no idea if they were secretly associated with the village of Al Quim or Al Qaeda. "What the hell did the Iraqi civilians need escorts for?" I thought. They lived in this godforsaken place and cursed every aspect of American life. Now, we had to drive their asses back to where we lived, right back to where I slept. I had no idea who these people were or whom they were associated with and yet I had to be okay and willing to protect them from all of the dangers of Iraq.

As This Lieutenant continued on, a guy behind me whispered to one of his buddies, "This bitch is fucking crazy to even think that we can make it back to Al Asad with these Iraqis and not run into some shit from the village." He said it loud enough in formation for a couple of us around him to turn and look. We all agreed with him, some of us rolling our eyes at This Lieutenant's decision, looking down at our boots to count the number of threads in our bootlaces, trying to mask the looks of disapproval on our faces.

She finished up the brief, asking if any of us had any questions about tonight's convoy. I wanted to conjure an objection about this convoy back to Al Asad. I thought that maybe if I suggested that the platoon didn't feel safe about tonight, that it was about to be 1900, that she was putting us all in an unnecessarily dangerous situation, she would change her mind and cave to the idea of staying at Al Quim for the night. Maybe I could just blatantly tell her she was out of her mind, with all due respect and that would also make her stay. But if I said anything to her along those lines, Staff Sergeant would chew me out and probably have me charged under military law for disrespect to an officer as soon as I got back to Al Asad. It would be the end of my career as I knew it. But I wanted to see war. I wanted to feel war. I wanted to experience every aspect of what a firefight felt like. The chance to fire my weapon tonight slowly put my almost raised hand in my pocket.

Into the night we journeyed back to Al Asad. The moon was closer than I had ever seen it. The desert night was silent, the hills standing in the dark as the wind blew softly. The engines of our trucks roared as the road turned and twisted past the cement factory, over the multiple IED holes, and entered the mouth of the village as the gates of the Al Quim base quickly disappeared into the black of the night. I moved my rifle closer to me so I could shorten the time it would take me to fire.

As I went to check my mirrors, I saw the rest of the convoy fall behind me as there were only four trucks ahead of me. One of the Iraqi truck drivers carrying supplies back to base with us had taken a wrong turn and the rest of the convoy had followed him. I tried to radio This Lieutenant but no signal. I attempted multiple times to radio in, holding the base of the antenna with force, hoping that it would create enough frequency. No response. Not even for two seconds. My gunner yelled at me from the turret to speed up toward the third truck. Every time I punched the gas, the third truck sped up to keep distance in case it ran over an IED and wouldn't take us out with it.

When we passed the entrance of the village, the three trucks in front of me slowed down enough to group up, enabling us to make our way through the village at a steady pace. I racked a round into the chamber of my rifle, pointing it out the driver side window with a hand on the steering wheel. I felt sweat drip off my brow, my left hand clinging to the steering wheel while my right hand was underneath, pointing the rifle out toward the buildings. Excitement came over me though the nervousness of the situation made my hands tremble. It just seemed too quiet for anything bad not to happen. It was my chance, though, to fire my weapon and get my revenge. I had been waiting for this since I signed up for the Marines.

A shadow behind a cement barrier slowly slipped out between the chain link fence and concrete barrier. I couldn't make out his face but the shadow looked like a child, maybe eight to ten years old. He held something in his hand as he pointed at one of the truck in front of me. With the whip of his arm, he rolled something under one of the trucks. The gunner on the second truck, a guy named Dakota, peered through the opening in his gun turret to watch the item's path. It rolled fast enough underneath his truck as Dakota attempted to look closer over his turret, the item exploded as shards of metal went in all directions.

Another explosion quickly followed with more force. I didn't realize how real this all felt until the second explosion. At first, it felt like a training exercise. All the preparation for a moment like this, all the times I mentally went through thinking about how I would shoot my weapon, how I would empty multiple ammo cartridges, shooting and killing the enemy, had not have prepared me for how scared I felt. My ass cheeks clenched as I pulled the trigger of my rifle as fast as my finger could, shooting in the direction of the blast. I slammed the gas pedal of the truck as the engine roared at my feet. I whipped the truck hard into a left turn while red tracer rounds lit up the night sky.

Dakota whipped his .50 cal machine gun towards the small boy. The boy made eye contact with Dakota's barrel. His eyes lit up as if he had seen a ghost as his head swiveled quick to his right, looking for an escape route. The boy pumped his arms in furious motion as his feet followed. For the next few seconds, it seemed the interaction between Dakota and the small boy was in slow motion. The boy ran for his life as Dakota aimed in on him, Dakota's eyes and war face behind the power of the machine gun.

I wanted this kid dead. The combat-hungry part of me wanted him to be the first casualty of our unit. I wanted him to be made an example to the villagers of Al Quim that our unit was not to be fucked with anymore. No more throwing rocks at us, no more cursing in Arabic or we will kill you. But I felt something else during my want for blood. The human side of me, the little that was left, thought that if Dakota kills this kid, blood will always be on his hands. I would've watched a young boy die in front of me. I would have had the image of his death etched in my mind. I would have to live with that.

The kid ran faster and faster. Dakota racked back the charging handle loading a round into the chamber, the butterfly-shaped trigger of the gun grasped firmly in his hands. He locked onto the kid. Everything was in alignment for Dakota. There was no wind to make any adjustments. Dakota had a loaded gun. It was all perfect.

Just when I thought Dakota was going to get his kill, and my memory would be scarred, the kid vanished. He disappeared behind the concrete barriers and off into the maze of buildings and shadows. The look of frustration on Dakota's face never showed so boldly. His chance had passed. Dakota grabbed his rifle, holstering it into his right shoulder, searching for the kid, hoping he would pop out behind the barriers for a second chance. The boy never did.

I heard the radio suddenly work as we pushed through the village, firing rounds as we went. I was able to hear This Lieutenant say to meet at a rendezvous point two kilometers outside of the village. The rest of the convoy was still far behind and hadn't entered the village yet. I hoped that they wouldn't have to go through what our trucks did. All the time I wanted to see combat quickly turned into a wish I never wanted. It was all about my legacy. I wanted to fight. I wanted to see hell firsthand. Instead of validation and excitement, I felt anger and fear that I had almost died.

I jumped out of my truck at the rendezvous point, removing my Kevlar helmet and throwing it sharply at my truck. The

Assistant Convoy Commander stopped his Humvee, opening the door to see if we were okay. He didn't know that the eight of us in the four trucks had been attacked. He just asked me why I was so mad. I didn't bother to tell him that we were attacked by a grenade-throwing kid with small arms fire coming at us from all directions. I just told him that our radio didn't work and it upset me. I'm sure he found out later from the others what had happened but for the couple of minutes we were waiting for the rest of the convoy to regroup with us, I was waiting for This Lieutenant to come check on me so I could rip her face off.

She later came up to us, walking out of her passenger door as if nothing major had happened. Stepping towards us, she just asked if we were okay and if our radio was working, since she said she couldn't hear us. I wanted so badly to scream at her. The audacity she had to ask me if I was okay after the explosions and the tracer rounds overhead. I'm sure I wasn't the only one who wanted to kick her ass but I was so overcome with mixed emotions that I didn't say much to her at all. There were no words to describe my thoughts, my emotions, and my fear. All I could say was "Yes, ma'am, I'm fine."

The rest of the convoy joined back up with us and after a quick accountability check, all of us mounted into our trucks and proceeded back to Al Asad. My gunner didn't say much to me but I could've sworn I heard him swear out loud while we were headed back. Maybe he was cussing or crying like I wanted to. I didn't bother ever to ask him if he was okay. I didn't even bother to ask myself if I was okay. The incident in the village shook me. Combat was nothing I imagined it would be. I imagined it would be me charging toward the enemy, shooting rounds at them while my gunner would lay down suppressive fire from the machine gun. But what it ended up being was a little boy who took it upon himself to try to blow us up. It ended up with me debating about a boy rolling a grenade toward us and if I was ok to shoot him the next time it happened. The village incident represented what combat was now, small children and explosives against the most elite fighting force in the world.

The sky was dark and the base was eerily quiet as we got back to Al Asad late that night. I jumped out of my truck, not saying anything to anyone. I saw Dakota, enraged and full of anger. He dismounted his gun and threw it off the truck into the sand. His anger over not pulling the trigger was strong. He stormed off into the night back to the barracks, cursing and kicking the sand beneath his feet. The rest of the tour, he was more aggressive, antsy to pull the trigger on our future convoys. It was all he ever talked about, how he wanted to kill that boy and didn't. Dakota got to see small glimpses of combat a couple of more times. He was entranced by the art of killing. It was more important to him than anything. He even applied to stay out in Iraq another year after our tour was done. He got denied due to some reason the Marine Corps gave him. He said the reason he wanted to stay was for the money and the job of being on the convoys wasn't as hard as it was made out to be. To me, it seemed that after the night with the kid at Al Quim, it ignited a fire within him. There was something about pulling the trigger and having enemies' bodies fall at the hands of his rifle that appealed to him. That one kid at Al Quim changed Dakota forever.

After I cleaned my truck out, I grabbed the last cigarette out of my rucksack and walked over to the far side of the motor pool away from everyone. I wanted to be alone. I needed to have the events of this night register in my brain. I had seen the face of death tonight in the eyes of Dakota and a boy willing to die. I had fired my weapon just like I hoped to. I didn't kill anyone like I hoped to. Yet the cigarette in my hand trembled. I had explosions around me while rounds sporadically flew over my truck. I managed to drive away from the chaos without a scratch. I started to feel the tears roll down my cheeks as I no longer could keep my fear inside.

A voice asked me, "You all right, man?" It was Scarecrow, a guy who was one of the combat-seasoned Marines in our unit. He was here during the initial invasion in 2003 and had seen his share of combat. He knew what happened, he could sense it. I looked at him, tears flooding my eyes as I tried hard to hold them back. The sound of his voice was calm and collected. The wrinkles etched on his face illuminated every firefight he encountered his first time out in Iraq. He laid a hand on my shoulder as he attempted to calm me down.

"Yeah, I'm good man, just smoking a cigarette." I said to him.

Scarecrow pointed at my cigarette in my hand. "Liguori, you haven't even lit it yet."

He pulled out a Marlboro Red, stuck it in his mouth, and reached for his lighter. I proceeded to do the same but he lit mine before his smoke. He started to chuckle a bit as if he was reminiscing about the first time he had been attacked. He sat next to me, letting out a grunt as his knees lowered him to the dirt. The smoke traveled upward through the air as we both sat in a moment of silence.

"It was your first time, huh?" he said. I nodded my head in agreement as the cigarette between my fingers loosely sat. As I sat there with my head hung low, Scarecrow told me something that to this day I would never forget.

"You only live once. There are only so many times that you can face death and escape. There are only so many times that you can truly be thankful to God that you are able to smoke this cigarette right here and now. You have seen the worst side of life, the side that civilians can never see. They will never understand that. That's why you are who you are." We didn't say a word to each other after that.

There was no need to talk about it any further. We just sat there, quietly looking at the stars smoking our cigarettes.

FAITH

I WORE A ROSARY ON MY FLAK JACKET EVERY time I went outside the wire. It was given to me by my five year-old brother, who told me that Jesus would help protect me in Iraq. He had no idea what faith meant or what dangers I was heading off to face, but he firmly believed in his innocence that Jesus would protect me in whatever battle I came across. I hoped that this crucifix would keep me safe, armed, and full of aggression.

When things got rough, I wore it around my neck even when I was on base which was the safest place out in Iraq. At times I would sleep with it clutched in my hands, hoping that what my brother said was true, that Jesus would protect me. I clenched it close to my chest and at night when I would have cold sweats, I would be at ease when I saw Jesus dangling close to my heart.

The night at the Al Quim village, I walked back to the barracks by myself after Scarecrow and I talked. His words comforted me a little while I smoked that cigarette with him, but my mind was still struggling with tonight's events. My gear felt heavier than before. My eyes were dry from crying. As I entered my room, I slowly stripped off my gear and uniform and headed to the showers. Mostly everyone was in bed already and I had the showers all to myself. The water hit the back of my head as I stood beneath the shower head. I hoped that the water would wash away tonight's events. I wished that it would take all my fear and anxiety away and renew my strength. I thought about my crucifix, about how all the times I went to the church I believed that God and Jesus would take care of it, no matter what. But after tonight's events, my beliefs in God didn't make sense like they used to.

I turned the hot water off and dried off with my olive-colored towel. It was 0230 as I walked back to my rack completely alone. I was somewhat emotionally unstable, failing to grasp any sort of reason in what I had seen. The kid throwing the grenade at us, the explosions, the rounds, everything felt surreal.

I sat on my rack, about to climb into my sleeping bag, hoping a good night's sleep would deter my fears when I noticed the crucifix that hung on my flak jacket. After convoys, I usually felt relieved I was safe and off the road. But as I stared at the crucifix on my jacket, I started to think that maybe God had nothing to do with my protection. What I saw tonight was something that I thought would never exist in God's world. What I experienced was more concrete than believing in God, whom I have never seen or felt. I was told by my father and pastors, and the sermons they gave that God was there, I just had to believe he existed. But there was no way that kind of evil and atrocity could exist in a world he created.

Maybe God isn't real, I thought. Maybe the training the Marines gave me and the months of preparation were the reasons I survived. The Marines were real to me. War was real to me. God had not shown himself in a time where death had crossed my face. I undid the crucifix from my jacket and held it in my hand. I held my cross in the silence of the room. I let it run through my fingers, feeling all its plastic details with my thumb. I looked closely at the etching of Jesus. I took the crucifix, wrapped it as neatly as I could, and placed it inside my sea bag. It was hard for me to let go of this personal gift from my brother, but the crucifix didn't mean to me what it used to. I felt I only could protect myself with my rifle and machine guns, not God. I closed my eyes and drifted to sleep. In the morning, I grabbed my rifle and was ready for the next convoy while the crucifix stayed behind.

MOUSE

KYLE WATSON AND I WERE BOTH ON BARRACKS duty for the fourth night in a row and already boredom had taken over. I wanted to go back out on the convoys, but since my hand was broken from an ammunition boxing dropping on top of it during a convoy, I could not shoot or even drive. I just had to sit, on duty, in a chair, reading the same damn *Maxim* from some time ago. Kyle slowly moved the paper ball hockey puck with a broom handle, announcing his moves in an imaginary game between the Chicago Black Hawks and the San Jose Sharks. I joined him by standing in front of the barracks' entrance playing goalie. I felt like a kid again, playing hockey in the middle of the neighborhood street with my best friend. Going against Kyle's wrist and slap shots made me forget my broken hand.

He fired multiple shots at me and I deflected each one in hockey fashion, reaching my hand out for a glove save or kicking my legs awkwardly to stop a low shot to the right corner. Kyle backed up the ball, preparing for a slap shot, raising the broom handle high as possible without hitting the ceiling. He was saving this big shot for me to prove that all of his bragging about playing hockey back home in Chicago was the real deal. The broom cocked back, as Kyle turned his torso, swinging his arms down like a pendulum, and thrust forward the broom with great force. As Kyle made contact, a small mouse crossed paths with the broom and was catapulted towards me, along with the ball.

The paper ball traveled as far as paper could, being nearly weightless, while the mouse slipped by me for the first goal of the night. The window glass shattered as I looked behind me to find the small mouse bleeding, lying on its side. The mouse lay dead on the floor as Kyle and I looked at each other in bewilderment. Neither of us said anything. We both laughed, in complete shock that a mouse became a casualty as a result of the hockey game. I stood looking at every inch of it saying to myself, "Oh, well, a mouse died. Fucking throw it away."

Kyle picked the mouse up, threw it outside without any sort of burial or memorial, and walked back inside like it had never happened. I was more worried about how we were going to tell First Sergeant about breaking a damn window than we were about how a mouse was killed in a game of hockey. First Sergeant came out of his room at the end of the hallway, slamming the door behind him as he made his way towards the duty desk at the front entrance. He stared at both of us with a penetrating look. He stood tall over us as we cowered out of fear he would chew our asses all night long.

"Watson, Liguori, I don't want to even know what the fuck you were doing. Whatever it was, it better be cleaned up now."

I try to interject during First Sergeant's talk by explaining an innocent casualty of a hockey game but First Sergeant raised his right index finger in my face.

"Liguori, shut the fuck up before you say anything!"

I tried hard to keep my bearing even though deep down I wanted to burst out into laughter. Kyle Watson was smiling from ear to ear even though he was trying to keep his bearing as well. I thought First Sergeant was going to chew our asses, his spit hitting our face while his hands and arms moved in rapid motions. I was sure that he was going to tell us how dumb we must be to fuck around on duty. First Sergeant did neither of those. He didn't yell or scream. He stared right through us with his eyes and smirked a little out of the left corner of his mouth. First Sergeant knew he would have goofed off had he been on duty. He left us with a verbal warning that consisted of "Next time you two fuck around like this, you will be scrubbing the deck for the next two weeks with toothbrushes. Got it?"

We nodded our heads in agreement as First Sergeant stormed off to his room. We started to whisper amongst ourselves as Kyle swept up the glass and put the broom back in the closet. Kyle shut the closet door and out of nowhere raised his voice and said, "Buzz Lightyear to the rescue."

I burst into laughter and so did Kyle, as I held my sides while I lay on the floor. First Sergeant opened his door furiously and marched directly at us, stomping his feet on the linoleum floor. This time, I was sure First Sergeant was going to pick us up both by the collar and kick our asses. He looked pissed beyond belief. There was no humor behind his smirk, no verbal warning.

As First Sergeant demanded for us to stand at attention with our feet at a 45 degree angle and thumbs along our trouser seams, he brought his face inches away from ours. Beads of sweat started to form on his brow, his teeth white as plaster. I knew the ass-chewing of ass-chewings was going to happen to both of us. He stood taller than before, pressing his chest in the middle of where we were standing. He wedged his face between us, where Kyle's right ear and my left were positioned perfectly where First Sergeant could yell at both of us. When I thought I lose my hearing in my left ear, First Sergeant whispered to us.

"I don't look like Buzz Lightyear. Don't ever call me that again."

He laughed soft in our ears, slapped us simultaneously in the shoulders and walked back to his room. He didn't come out the rest of night. Kyle and I stood there in shock. We were still at attention, our feet at a 45 degree angle, and our thumbs along the trouser seams.

POEM

AFTER I HAD COME BACK FROM A CAMP HIT convoy, I walked with Kyle to the chow hall talking with him about girls and how we couldn't wait to give them all a piece of us when we deployed back to the U.S. We walked into the Chow Hall as it was packed with all the different units on base. There were multiple Army units overtaking two large rows, Marine units gathered in the back corner, even some of the Navy Seabee units had a small group near the front entrance. The Chow Hall was the only place where every unit on base could sit and eat at the same time. The food wasn't great, but seeing all different types of people from all over the U.S., serving their country made the experience worth it. Just as we sat down, I ran into Spider. Spider, in his southern drawl, yelled my name and waved me over with a wiggle of his middle and index finger. I responded back with a little wave of my hand, but he insistently waved me over.

"Hey, man, get your ass over here. I got something to ask ya!"

Spider viewed me like family. He had even tried to hook me up with his stepdaughter because he viewed me as a potential son-in-law. It didn't work out between me and his stepdaughter. She and I agreed on mutual terms that it wasn't going to work out for a lot of reasons. Spider understood when I told him about our mutual agreement but later told me that it was her fault and she was to blame for it not working.

I walked over to where Spider was sitting as I lay my food tray down across from him.

"So I hear it's your birthday in a couple days?" He said.

"What about my birthday?" I replied. "Not a whole lot you can do out in Iraq to celebrate your 21st birthday."

"I'm headed to Dubai with the boys for a couple days. Since your birthday is coming up, if you want something to drink, I can bring you something back."

My eyes lit up as it was some of the best news I had gotten so far being in Iraq.

"Hell, yeah, I want something to drink. Grab me some Jack Daniels and I'll be happier than shit."

"You got it, bud. I'll make sure I bring you back a big ol' bottle."

He laughed a little behind his thick mustache. I didn't really know what to say to him except laugh back. Not only was I getting alcohol from Spider in a place where it was as rare as a hot girl showing up at your door but I was going to be able to celebrate my 21st like I would back home.

A couple of days passed and I agreed to meet Spider at his tent about one kilometer from where I was staying. We weren't even supposed to be over there at all. Our command banned us from interacting with the civilian truck drivers. It probably had something to do with rumors of their gambling and heavy drinking. The truck drivers were notorious for having huge games of Texas Hold'Em, and I had heard some stories of huge amounts of money lost by Marines in other units who played with them. The last thing our command needed was to have a Marine lose all his money gambling or be drunk with a rifle and ammo in his possession.

Whenever you walked over to Spider's tent, it felt like an old western saloon with Hank Williams, Johnny Cash, and Conway Twitty playing from the radios with cigarette smoke permeating the air and chew cans scattered across the floor. Spider was sitting at the table, legs crossed, with a big 'ole chew in his lower lip. A brass spittoon sat on his right side, bottles of water and beef jerky wrappers along the head of his bed. He signaled for me to come toward his rack. He rocked the chair forward as he grabbed his backpack. Spider opened the front pouch and pulled an Arizona Ice Tea bottle with multiple layers of tape on top of the lid

"So I got you that bottle you asked for," he said with a smirk. "You should take some shots before you go back to the barracks. It is your birthday and I did drive to Dubai to get your ass some whiskey. Least you can do is have a shot with me"

"Well, to be honest, I would polish off the whole bottle with you but I don't want to get caught with it on my breath. We aren't even allowed to be over here anyway and I get caught with whiskey on my breath, I'm screwed."

Kyle grabbed the bottle as Spider went to hand it to me.

"Liguori, stop being a bitch! It's your damn birthday. You can have one shot. Be a patriot dammit!"

He was right. It was my birthday. One shot wasn't going to hurt. I could chew a shitload of gum, smoke some cigarettes, and no one would know. Plus, guys in Vietnam were getting drunk to pass time and deal with the shit they saw every day, like the bodies of dead Viet Cong bent in lifeless poses. I hadn't seen any Hajjis bent life-less, but my close encounters with IED's and kids throwing rocks at me were more than a reason to have a few shots.

"All right, pour me a shot. It is my birthday," I replied as I looked for a shot glass.

"Well, now that you agreed to drink, the hell you are taking just one shot." Spider said. "You better finish that whole bottle before you leave. I had to go all the way to Dubai just to get that shit. You'd be drinking that Canadian Whiskey crap the Hajjis try to sell you, if it weren't for me."

Spider pulled some chairs up for us as he grabbed both Kyle and me cups for our drinks. We toasted our cups as Spider started to talk about his time in the first Gulf War as a young Marine. He told us the weeks he spent in Desert Storm were a bunch of bullshit just like this one. We started telling him stories of the convoys and how the Marine Corps was this day and age. The story-swapping turned into drinking and talking shit of who could drink the most.

Kyle and I decided to head back to the barracks though we were both buzzed. I took the bottle with me, making sure the tape on the bottle cap was sealed tight, so I didn't spill anything in my pant pocket. On our walk back, Kyle and I took small sips, acting like we were in high school, hiding the bottle from cops looking for underage drinkers. The sips hit me so hard as it took me longer than expected to grab the door handle and walk through the back of the barracks. I couldn't stop laughing and neither could Kyle as we felt the whiskey hit us all at once.

I announced to everyone in my room it was my birth-day and I had a surprise as I pulled the bottle out from my cargo pant pocket. Guys gravitated toward the bottle, tak-ing swigs and passing it around to the others. Minutes lat-er, the bottle was empty, lying on the floor as everyone in my room was completely drunk. It was like a huge frat party except without the wasted freshman girls stumbling around in the hallways. We jumped around and screamed at the top of our lungs like we were at a heavy metal concert.

One of the guys put in a DVD named *Bum Fights*. It was one of our favorites, due to its extremely violent to bizarre scenes with homeless people they paid to do crazy things. Kyle watched one scene where a homeless man read a foul, offensive poem at an open mic night. He quickly pushed the rewind button, grabbing a pen and paper. He rewound the DVD numerous times and sat copying every uncouth word.

"I'm going to go read this to Gunny," said Kyle, his eyes wide as he started to laugh.

"Kyle, you can't, dude. We're going to get busted," I said. If anyone was going to keep Kyle from bringing any attention to us, it was me. I didn't like to be in trouble even though somehow trouble always found me, especially when I hung around Kyle. The last thing I needed was to be an accomplice in one of Kyle's antics considering whiskey was now involved.

"Who gives a shit, Liguori? Every motherfucker in here needs to loosen up. Stop being a little bitch." Kyle pushed my shoulder as he flipped over a piece of yellow paper. Kyle finished copying the poem, every line written down in his chicken scratch. My birthday went from an exclusive gathering of Spider, Kyle and me toasting to another year of life to half of my platoon drunk, yelling and playing Xbox.

Both of us walked outside to the smoke pit where Gunny and the Captain were smoking Cuban cigars.

"Excuse me, Gunny?" Kyle interrupted them. "I would like to read a poem I wrote for you."

"It better not be some girly shit, Watson! Last thing I need to hear is any sappy bullshit coming out of your mouth," Gunny replied.

The Captain muttered, "Well, actually, to be frank with you, Gunny, I encourage him to read whatever he has. Go ahead, Watson."

The Captain was somewhat of a nerd. He thoroughly enjoyed school and many of his speeches to us were filled with encouragement to enroll in college and to learn everything we could about the Marines.

As I held my breath hoping Gunny wouldn't smell the whiskey, Kyle read the entire poem, speaking each vulgar word with feeling and emotion. By the end of the poem, the Captain looked at both of us appalled. He squinted, rubbing his face with apparent disgust, while Gunny laughed his ass off. But Gunny's laughter stopped as he realized the Captain was not pleased with Kyle's masterful poem. He didn't say anything in response to the poem, just put out his cigar and walked inside the barracks. Gunny quickly followed the Captain back inside. Kyle and I attempted to gather some military bearing, standing at attention even though the smoke pit spinning made it hard to keep our balance. We watched the Captain speak to Gunny in a calm demeanor. He didn't seem mad; maybe Kyle's poem was humorous to the Captain, I thought. Kyle nudged me and nodded his head to the side, signaling that maybe it was time for us to leave.

When we were about to make our exit and get back to our room, Gunny swung the door opened and yelled.

"You two get your asses over here now!!"

Immediately, we did an about-face and rushed to Gunny's position. He told us to stand at attention as he informed he was going to get First Sergeant.

"You two must be dumb as shit to read something that offensive to the Company Commander." Gunny's eyes opened up as his pupils shrunk to pinpoints. His jaw clenched, wanting to unleash an ass chewing from hell on us. He walked over and knocked on First Sergeant's room. First Sergeant opened the door, standing in his sweatpants and flip-flops as Gunny told him about the poem Kyle had written.

"I'm not surprised Gunny that it is these two knuckleheads. Go again, Watson. Read your damn poem for me."

Kyle was forced to read the poem again while I stood next to him with my head down trying not to laugh. First Sergeant laughed his ass off during the poem. But soon, his laugh dried up and he put on a straight face as he found out from Gunny that we had read the poem to the Captain. First Sergeant towered over us, just like before. Though Gunny was shorter than First Sergeant, he somehow managed to make me feel I was barely five feet. The spit and rapid hand arm movements from both of them were intimidating. They both screamed at the top of their lungs as others from the unit peered out into the hallway to see what the screaming was about.

After the double team ass-chewing, Gunny and First Sergeant looked at us silently. They stared right through us. I was scared to have them find out we had been drinking. The closer they moved their faces, the more I felt like caving into telling them we had whiskey. They waited for us to break down and tell them. But Kyle and I never did. We did the best we could to keep military bearing even though we were partly smiling through the ass-chewing and the stare-down. Gunny and First Sergeant looked at each other, nodding their heads in agreement. They turned their faces towards us and with little smiles, told us their verdict.

"Both of you have will be busy the next two weeks."

"Yes Gunny. Yes, First Sergeant."

Kyle and I saw that inside both First Sergeant and Gunny were laughing, and knew we were drunk. They still had to enforce rules; just like fathers who found out their kids had done something so ridiculous it made them laugh, but still had to discipline them. So for the next two weeks, we had police call duty. And we had motor pool night duty. And we had barracks duty. And we had to write an apology note to the Captain for the poem and our behavior. But it was my twenty-first birthday and it was well worth it.

HEARTACHE

A FRIEND OF MINE HAD THE WORST LUCK of all when it came to love. Greg was a nice kid, had a good heart and everything. His front teeth stuck out a little every time he spoke, kind of like Goofy. He was always the one guy who no matter how down on his luck he was, he would always look forward to the next day. That was his personality, someone who saw the good in everything. He didn't mind Iraq; he didn't mind being away from his girlfriend, because he believed he would go back to see her.

Greg planned on marrying her when he got back. He loved her more than anything. The three years they had together, he told me, were some of the best years of his life. They talked for hours on the phone while we were out in Iraq. He cried because he missed her and laughed because she kept his mind off the monotony of convoys. She was there for him when he needed it. It was love, pure and natural as it could be. He was tempted to marry her before he left, not as a contract marriage, but because it just felt right. But the deployment came upon him quick, forcing him to leave earlier than expected from his reserve station. This love was real to him. It got him through the days where the convoys were long and treacherous. The love he shared with his girlfriend was everything to him.

One day he received the most dreaded piece of mail any one could ever receive while being deployed. His girlfriend sent him a "Dear John" letter, explaining to him that the long tours to Iraq and the void he had left every time he was deployed over the past three years were more than he could expect her to handle. She had gone into the relationship hoping each tour was the last tour for him, so he could be home and life afterward for them would be able to start. Like all of us, the needs of the Marine Corps were greater than those of the individual. Greg always agreed to deployments out of his love for the Marines and every time he left his reserve station, he knew he was going to come back. He just never knew that she wouldn't be there.

She had emptied his bank account, hooked up with their apartment manager, and ran away with him to another state. He never heard from her again. The money, apartment and his pride were cleaned out. Even some of the furniture was gone. When Greg called home looking for answers, his buddies told him about his apartment, empty and abandoned just as he was.

He clutched the letter tightly in his grip as his eyes read the paper, scanning each line with precision. He absorbed each word. I wanted to put my arm around him and comfort him during his heartache, but I kept to myself. Putting my arm around him would have done little for what he was feeling right then. I stood by him, thinking of what I could say.

He resisted the tears that wanted to stream down his face. He wanted to cry and he had every right, too. But he never did cry after that letter like he should've. He just got up from sitting on his rack and walked outside to the back of the barracks. Iraq, along with that letter, had drained him of emotion.

THE SANDBOX

After that letter, Greg went around putting up the façade of a motivational, "gung-ho" Marine. He stayed late at the motor pool to work. He cleaned his rifle constantly, even volunteered to clean the machine guns in the armory after convoys. But the days where he smiled all the time, always tilting his head toward the sun, disappeared. All he talked about was how excited he was to get on another convoy and hope to shoot his weapon. Greg was never the same after the letter; he was too far involved in the war to deal with it.

After our tour, I imagined him coming home to his empty apartment, finding a yellow note sitting on the bed, crinkled at the corners with the words, "I love you and I am sorry, but I couldn't do it anymore" scribbled lightly on it. I pictured him sitting with his head hung low between his legs, completely silent, remembering Iraq forever mixed up with his heartache. He had served his country honorably. Greg went back to Iraq because he thought it was the right thing to do. He thought if he served his country, his girlfriend would understand. She didn't though. She thought of the Marines as another woman that Greg had secretly been having an affair with behind her back. His sacrifice and commitment to the Marines ended up sacrificing their relationship.

Greg's heart-breaking experience tore me up inside. He was betrayed to his very soul by the girl he loved, who took her love away from him and gave it to someone else, like he gave his love to his country and the Marines. She gave it to someone who was there while Greg was in Iraq. That was the kind of heartache I didn't want any part of. I saw why guys went overseas single with no drama attached to them. It was all business: no deep emotional connections. There was no need to explain the love for the Marines or for their country to someone who wasn't in their position. There was no need to justify serving. Marines are trained to fight. It's their primary responsibility. Everything else is second when it comes to that.

PILGRIMAGE

OUR UNIT WAS GIVEN THIS MISSION to help support the Hajj, which is the pilgrimage to Mecca, Saudi Arabia that Muslims make at least once in their lifetime to fulfill their religious duty to serve Allah. The mission didn't sit too well with us, especially since violence in the region had escalated. The Hajj was going to involve hundreds of thousands of Muslims and the concentration of insurgents was likely to be very high. Usually, our unit insisted on being vigilant and aggressive, searching for targets and being first to shoot the moment we felt the least bit threatened. But since the US deemed our support of the pilgrimage as a humanitarian effort, our unit couldn't be as aggressive as we wanted to be. We would have to be defensive, not threatening towards the people of the Hajj.

It was upsetting for me at first, when I was told we were just going to bring water to an abandoned UN outpost on the border of Iraq and Saudi Arabia. Here we were strapping loads of water to our trucks, making sure that every cargo strap tightly fastened would hold all 124 pallets while we traveled the next three days to the border instead of preparing ourselves for possible firefights. I felt our chances for survival were hampered if we were to be non-threatening and defensive. It made us more susceptible to being blown up or shot at. But the more I thought about it, the more I saw it as a chance for me not to have to look for my first kill.

Maybe by having this mission be a humanitarian effort, the chance for violence would decrease and I could be peaceful, get to know the people of the Hajj without having to worry about being blown up or shot. I could see them as people rather than see them as possible hostile threats. It was my chance to extend my hand in friendship. But I was still in Iraq, still in a combat zone where any moment kindness or peacefulness is shown, death is likely to follow.

We stopped at a rural Iraqi police station. We exited our vehicles to line up on the side of the road and huddled together for a smoke break. While part of our convoy was being off-loaded, I saw in the distance kids running around hand in hand, following their mothers like ducks in a row. They sang songs and burst out in joyous laughter. Women and children were a good sign. When they were out, the chances of getting fired at decreased significantly. Seeing mothers hold their children's hands, singing joyfully, was comforting.

The smoke in my hand slowly burned as I watched another group of kids run in circles, passing a soccer ball amongst them. I wanted to play soccer with them, take a break from the monotony of the combat zone. I wanted to have them pass the ball to me so I could show them some tricks. I wanted to walk over to the kids and let them see my hands, how I had wrinkles making their way horizontally across them. My hands, when uncurled from clenched fists, were gentle and caring. I wanted to show them peace.

But I was on a convoy. I still had to be vigilant. I was in a more dense area than Al Quim, and dropping my weapon to show my hands to the children could've gotten me killed. The warrior in me came back to the surface as I threw my smoke on the ground and clutched my rifle with both hands. The feelings of openness and kindness were pushed down as the aggression and numbness I regularly felt were again strong. I aimed my rifle slightly towards the kids I had hoped to friend.

After the off-load, we packed up and headed back out onto the second part of our journey to Camp Mudaysis. I had never been to Mudaysis, but heard from those that had that it was a bitch to get there. We still had a couple of hours to go before we got there and the farther we traveled to the camp, the more desolate the terrain became. There were no more buildings standing out against the flat ground or kids running through the desert. The only things running free-spirited, like the children at the police station, were the random camels that strayed away from their packs while looking for water. They seemed like they were minding their own business. As we passed them, the camels looked at our trucks like, "What the hell you doing out here?" Their fixed eyes upon on us just long enough to give us the impression that they weren't stupid. I looked right at them and whispered to myself, "I'm wondering the same thing, buddy."

Mudaysis looked like a tiny replica of something out of a Star Wars movie. The buildings were molded out of clay. The muddy earth that supported this small camp in the middle of nowhere was probably the reason "Mudaysis" seemed such a fitting name. The long ride made my ass fall asleep in the driver's seat and once we dismounted from the trucks to start our off-load, I felt the rush of blood push through my legs. I hated having my ass and legs fall asleep from driving so much, but my job was to drive, and personal discomfort always took a backseat to the mission.

Tired and exhausted, I walked into the Chow Hall, dragging my feet across the ground, kicking up sand behind me. I pushed the wood swinging door open and was greeted by four hot pans of food. Powdered Gatorade was the drink special for tonight, along with chicken and potatoes. I never wondered how the chicken was prepared, or if the potatoes were boiled or microwaved, I was just happy that I got something to eat. I was used to not eating tasty meals, or home-cooked ones for that matter. Trust me, after not having my favorite home-cooked meal or any meal worth stomaching for a couple of months, chicken and potatoes sounded amazing.

Sometimes I liked sitting by myself when I ate. I didn't mind being alone and dinner was a time to sit quietly and reflect. As my food cooled, I fought my own mental battle with the war. It was hard traveling all these miles and not knowing when the next IED was going to hit. The thoughts of "if I died in a combat zone" came up when I was alone. I tried hard not to think about my death, since, well, I was alive. But it was hard not to. It was hard not to think if your family would miss you and who would come to your funeral. It was hard not to think about when death was a possibility every day. Yet, thinking of my possible death led me to enjoy the little things in life, such as breathing, smokes, and the chicken dinner at the Chow Hall. It let me appreciate the ability to have the mental battles.

Sitting alone helped me observe the behaviors and mannerisms of Marines in the desert without being distracted by direct conversation. I saw how they talked to each other while one of them would dump pepper or salt into the other one's food, hoping to play a practical joke. I saw guys with arms around each other, smiling as if the world couldn't have been better than where they were right now. Their minds were not in Mudaysis. They were off in a beach in Hawaii, having the time of their lives. Sitting at the table with their fellow Marines was pure. The mental rigors of war, the thoughts of when death would approach them, were gone. There were no discussions about religion or political beliefs, just smiles and laughter. There were no talks about why the U.S. was fighting in Iraq. There was no anger or aggression. All that came out at that dinner was family.

They didn't have enough beds for our unit, so we had to sleep outside on cots underneath the moonlight. A sleeping bag was all I needed, but it wouldn't have hurt to have a pillow or two. I got pretty good after a couple months at being thankful for whatever I was given. The little things, like a warm sleeping bag on a cold night like this, were better than sleeping with nothing at all. Even the moonlight shining on my face made me appreciate the gift of taking breaths of cold winter air.

Right before I went to sleep, a buddy of mine asked if I wanted to come hang out for a bit with the rest of the platoon. Even though my eyes were heavy and my body heat had just started to fully circulate in my sleeping bag, I agreed to come join them. The cold was brutal but not enough to keep me from spending time with the others.

After seconds of preparing my mind and body to get out of my sleeping bag, I finally grabbed my boots, sliding my feet in them without tying the bootlaces. In full sweats and combat boots, I broke into a slow, sloppy jog over to the shadows where people were huddling close to a small fire. The small circle was filled with guys standing shoulder to shoulder, not only to keep warm but to conceal a bottle of whiskey that someone opened. One of the guys had it sent to him before the battalion-mandated care package checks to stop alcohol being sent to our unit. It was wrapped neatly in newspaper, cradled in one of the guy's arms like a newborn. When opened, it smelled pure and clean of fresh U.S. alcohol, the "good shit," as I always referred to it. As the bottle was passed around, each one of us took a large sip, grimacing after the whiskey went down our throats. Alcohol made us forget the lack of hot water, home cooked meals, and the love of a woman. Despite my frustration with the Hajj, the camaraderie of the Marines plus the bottle of alcohol were strong enough to get me through the night.

The bottle slowly diminished and we became more outgoing, telling stories, talking trash about each other's football teams. I enjoyed the conversation. I enjoyed being able to see guys kick their feet up on a rock or smoke a cigarette and share it with others. The calming feeling of alcohol warmed my throat on this cold winter evening. Every move that we made stood out in the spotlight of the moon. We laughed and drank until the alcohol made us sleepy and it was time to hit the rack. I walked back to my sleeping bag, watching the ground move slowly beneath my feet.

My boots came off, as well, and I folded my clothes neatly, or at least I think I folded them nicely. I gazed at the stars and admired how close they were to my face, like a little nightlight. I thought about how months ago I was in California and now I was sleeping on a cot in the middle of the desert. I was here with my brothers. Every single one of these men needed strength and support to carry on through the turmoil and hardships this place brings. Whenever I needed courage to live another day, the Marines of my unit gave me all I needed. I turned the top layer of the sleeping bag as I climbed in, zipping it closed as I fell asleep.

The next morning, I woke to my face feeling numb and saw a slight layer of frost casing the ground. That winter morning took the longest to get dressed, and everyone was late for accountability formation. No one wanted to get out of his sleeping bag due to the cold, and's last night's drinking festivities made staying in the sleeping bag more delightful than walking to chow.

After breakfast and accountability formation, we got in our trucks and headed to the border of Saudi Arabia and Iraq. We arrived a couple hours later at an old abandoned U.N. outpost on the border. The Iraqis on the receiving end of our delivery were waiting, looking like a pack of wolves. They stood in awe of our equipment as we towered over them in every way. Their once brave looks turned submissive when they saw the size of our shoulders and our weapons.

They waved their hands, signaling to off load the water near an empty lot where they were standing. Our trucks pulled into the lot and immediately we jumped out ready to undo all the cargo straps holding the water cases down. Once the straps started to come off, the Iraqis jumped onto the bed of the trucks, manually passing the cases down to the others. But they thought it was going to take too long to pass each case by hand and our unit didn't have time to be stuck overnight at the outpost. We had to be back to Al Asad in two days and we were running behind schedule.

Unexpectedly, the Iraqis got behind the giant pallets, pushing and kicking them over. All the countless hours of stacking each pallet one by one in a neat fashion was ruined by their mismanagement. We brought them water and they ended up pushing the huge pallets off the truck as the bottles exploded onto the ground. Even if they seemed grateful for us bringing them water, the way they off loaded it seemed like they could give a shit. I felt they took for granted that we had done this for them; they must have had a sense that we were forced to bring them water. They knew we regretfully brought them the water. They knew that if we had our way, the unit would have arrested every single one of them and brought them to Abu Gharib prison. It didn't even matter if they were innocent or not, the disrespect of the off load made me want to beat them down with the butt stock of my rifle.

During the off load, one of the Iraqi workers approached Dakota and attempted to trade his boots for Dakota's. The Iraqi's eyes were wide, and he was smiling from ear-to-ear, hoping Dakota would agree to swap with him. I felt Dakota's rage. I felt the disrespect he also felt from the way the Iraqis offloaded the water pallets. It was pretty ballsy of the Iraqi to pick Dakota, considering Dakota had turned from a small town kid from the Midwest into a shark searching for blood. The Al Quim incident had flipped a switch in him and I worried Dakota would see this as a chance to kill the guy.

But somehow Dakota managed to lower his guard around the man. He showed him kindness and willingness to listen to the offer. For a brief moment, Dakota had showed his humanity. Regretfully, he told the man that he couldn't trade with him due to unit regulations. I smiled to myself as I was no longer mad watching Dakota walk away back to his truck while the Iraqi worker stared at him with a smile. Dakota was human after all. He showed a glimpse of who he was before he entered combat. If a man as deeply enrooted in war as Dakota could show humanity to the Iraqis without fear of death then there was hope for peace.

After our unit delivered the water, we spent the next couple of days driving back to Mudaysis and from there back to Al Asad. Initially, I felt the Hajj was supposed to be this bullshit mission. I felt that this mission was some political move by the U.S. government to show the Iraqis we cared about them. Our unit anticipated ambushes or IED attacks. I waited for bad things to happen. I waited for rounds and mortars to rain down on our position. None of that happened.

The Hajj let me feel something: that in a war full of chaos and anger, a sliver of peace existed. It was small as an exchange between a battle-hardened Marine and a struggling, oppressed Iraqi or as large as a gathering at the dinner table. It even made itself known with the children at the police station. They continued to play despite the war in their country. They smiled and played as if nothing ever changed. They managed to kick a soccer ball in dirt fields surrounded by buildings filled with bullet holes.

ODE

IPROMISED MYSELF THAT IF I EVER HAD A chance to write my experiences and true feelings about the war, I would include my memories of my dear friend Joe. He embodied humor. His life revolved around finding the bright side of any situation. He wasn't the outspoken type and wasn't much of a conversationalist. He would give you shit in his honest attempt to make you laugh, or make you not feel that you were a complete failure when he did his drill instructor voice, yelling "Hello, you!!" Joe never disrespected anyone. His intentions were always about having a good time. During my worst times, the times where my second tour of Iraq was about to get the best of me, he would dance, arms pumping up and down in a mosh pit-like fashion, in every attempt to make me laugh at his antics and see that life was too short to be agonizing over the perils of war.

My friend Erik told me how Joe had helped him during his lowest point, when Erik's divorce had completely driven a nail through his soul. Joe took him out every other night for two months in order to distract his mind from the hard divorce. They spent hours on end discussing everything from girls they glanced at in the bars to how music allowed them to not feel pain. The band "Alice in Chains" had become their connection, the bond that made them both feel no pain as they listened to the powerful, somber voice of lead singer Layne Staley. They shared beers, moments, and thoughts over these songs and when Erik felt like all was lost, Joe gave him another chance at life.

Months after they had gotten back from their deployment in 2003, Erik was promoted to Sergeant. Erik accepted the promotion with honor, fully motivated to carry out his duties as best as he possibly could. It was exciting for him and meant everything to be a Sergeant of Marines. Joe knew that even though he was happy for Erik, it was the end of their great friendship. The Marine Corps didn't allow Marines of different rank to hang out with each other. Erik tried hard to keep their friendship strong but the responsibilities of having other Marines under his supervision were too great for him to continue his friendship with Joe. The nights where they drank, shared stories, and listened to Alice in Chains were far and few.

When our unit got home from Iraq after my second tour, we consumed large amounts of alcohol several times a week to celebrate a safe deployment. Of course, none of us at the time thought it was bad; we weren't doing anything that most 21 year-old kids were doing. Joe did it too. He started drinking like all of us.

Time went on after our unit deployed home safely and Joe attempted to take the partying to another level. It was like there was this binge drinking survival game, see who could drink and party the longest. At first, we all drank and celebrated our survival. As days and weeks passed, the pyramid shrank as some were still drinking. Eventually, the ones who drank daily were the minority at the top. Joe was one of them and even managed to single himself out by "huffing" computer duster to the point of unconsciousness. Joe would take the cans of computer duster he bought at the Public Exchange on base; head back to his room and inhale the contents of the can. At times, I would walk into Joe's room and see him passed out with multiple cans scattered on his floor. His habits became an issue for the unit but mostly among his friends. No one wanted to see him in the state he was in, an abuser of alcohol and huffing. I never wanted to see my friend slowly destroy himself.

Erik still did what he could, despite the fraternization rules, to make sure Joe didn't do anything to harm himself. He tried to talk to Joe about the duster and the drinking. He knew that his good friend was struggling with readjustment; Joe had lost his ability to be in the moment. I felt that Joe was the classic case of an emotionally distressed soldier who feels war alienated him from civilian life. Erik and I both tried to be there for him but the closer we got to him stopping, the farther he fell into his dark hole of alcohol and "huffing."

One day, while I was on duty, I found Joe passed out behind the steering wheel of his car in the barracks parking lot. I saw the cans of duster on the passenger seat and knew that things had taken a turn for the worse. He had wrecked multiple cars in the barracks while huffing on his way out. He didn't remember what had happened when he awoke and seemed paranoid when he saw cars wrecked were because of him huffing duster. He didn't remember how he got behind the wheel and how his car had taken damage. He denied he wrecked those cars but the evidence clearly pointed at him. I was so angry at him I couldn't yell or scream. In fact, I was so angry I couldn't even wrap my brain around what had happened. I wanted to protect him from getting in trouble but I just couldn't protect him from something like this. I just shook my head in shame as I waited for the Battalion Duty Watch to come down.

Joe got into trouble with the battalion for the parking lot incident. He was deemed a "shit bag" by some of the higher ups for his behavior. Erik and I knew he wasn't a shit bag by any means; Joe was clearly having emotional struggles and issues. He dealt with it through alcohol and computer duster. Every time he held nitrous to his mouth, it gave his mind a chance to breathe. The huffing had consumed him, eating away every last bit of his free soul.

Erik and I tried to save him. A lot of Joe's friends tried to intervene. Some of us were mandated by our unit to take turns on endless nights of suicide watch. Whenever I did suicide watch with Joe, I never felt I was watching him. It was a more like a chance to hang out with my friend. We would talk about everything, from music to video games. He was himself, no duster or alcohol. I didn't have to take things away from him or go searching for substances that could kill him. He reached out to me.

Joe was eventually discharged. I heard from some of his friends that he worked a couple jobs soon after and it seemed he was on his way to getting his life together. But the stress from the war, along with his deep emotional issues from his past, ate away his happiness and kept him from having any stability. He ended up alone, isolated from the world. Erik told me he was on his way to get Joe, bring him to Texas and help him get back on his feet. Erik was going to save Joe from his own demise, giving him another chance to live. But the drugs and alcohol were too much. It was all he had around him as the arms of God received him with open love.

When I heard Joe had passed, I remember the emptiness I felt. It was the emptiness you felt when regret hit you and made you feel more could have been done. The nights I stayed with him on suicide watch or the times it was just me and him hanging outside the tents in Al Taquddum, Iraq, I always used to ask if he was okay and he always gave me the hang ten signal with an "All good, man." The nights I spent with him were always full of great conversations and laughter. I tried to give him my own two cents about his behavior, hoping my advice would sink into his mind. The more I attempted to help him, the more I hoped he would come back from the depths of his own peril. I wish I could have saved him.

I miss his subtle jokes and the bags of Cool Ranch Doritos he used to have. I miss his laugh, his outlook on life, and how he was always about a good time. Erik and I, to this day, still talk about Joe and remember how important he was to us. If he were around me, physically, there would be at least of couple of chips falling to the floor as he attempted to cram a whole handful into his mouth, smiling as he failed with every attempt. It makes me smile knowing now Joe is in heaven and he is okay. I do wish though that Joe for one night could come down from heaven, open a bag of Doritos and ask me if I wanted any.

"In memory of this great soul who gave what he was able to give: He was a great mind and his leaving left a great void not only in my life but his friends and family who loved him. We honor him. Thanks for making our hearts feel love at times when it was hard to and teaching us all to smile. We miss you more than ever and thanks for being in our lives. Rest in paradise, my brother, and I will see you someday."

LUCK

SERGEANT "R" HAD RUN OVER A DOUBLE-stacked mine somewhere around Camp Hit and it just missed him, only to shatter the back of his truck. The windows were blown out as glass shards lay on the Kevlar seats. The canvas trap was ripped into small slivers just wide enough to let light into the truck. The truck had taken all the damage from the blast. He came away from that landmine completely unscathed, not a scratch on him.

After he had just driven in the gate to the motor pool, guys were shaking his hands and hugging him. First Sergeant even gave him a fatherly pat on the back. In a matter of hours, he went from a mechanic to a living legend. He just threw everyone a smile and "Thanks, man." A week later, he went out on another convoy and once again, another IED went off just after he swerved around it, the back tires on the passenger side tripping it. The vehicle was worse off than the first time. Once again, he walked away without a scratch. But the second IED hit his psyche hard and transformed him into an individual with no identity.

The day after, his normal loud mouth had escalated to screaming and yelling as he cussed young Marines out, over every slight irritation. He started smoking cigarettes more than ever. His work ethic was double, his motivation for the Corps was double, and his intake of caffeine and tobacco was double.

When I was on barracks duty, Sergeant R would walk out into the night, in a dark green sweatshirt and sweatpants with just a rifle slung over his back. His strife was fast and his fists were clenched. His trips into the night were more and more frequent. I didn't know where he went off to but I never saw him until the next day. I always wondered where he would go but when I would show up to the motor pool, there he was, covered in grease.

One night, I watched Sergeant R disappear out the back door. I decided to take a smoke break as I followed him, trying to stay far back enough that he wouldn't know I was following him. Gently, I shut the door making my way toward the port-a-johns. The night sky was dark and the lights on base were just enough to help me see where I was walking. I was determined to follow him, to see if he was okay and why he always disappeared into the night. As I made it past the port-a-johns, I stopped. I watched him in a slow jog disappear past the lights toward the direction of the motor pool into the dark of the night.

I pulled out a smoke from my chest pocket while my eyes were still fixated on his position. My curiosity over the proceeding weeks gradually ceased. I thought there was no need for me to trek him anymore. The man had been through a lot in the past weeks. Just like when I saw my first action, I speculated that he wanted to be alone.

After my smoke break, I came back inside and went to my rack. I felt reading a magazine or maybe a book might help put my worries at rest. I thought my fear of death and the unknown would subside if I looked at some scantily clad women in *Maxim*. As I went to grab them off my sea bag, a picture dropped onto the floor. I reached under my rack, curious to see what was enclosed, and felt the texture of a picture with the edges bent on all four sides.

I brought the picture from underneath my rack towards my eyes. I held the pictures' tattered edges as I stared at the picture. Here was a young man, full of Marine Corps bearing with his uniform pressed. A chiseled jawline with a clean shave and his hat slightly tilted toward the bridge of his nose. His stare showed that he was ready to fight a war at eighteen years of age. He had no idea what war entailed, what it meant to put his life on the line for others. He didn't know what it was like to be shot at, or survive multiple IED attacks like Sergeant R. The young man just knew that war was what he wanted. When it was time for him to go to war, he would experience it all and fight with every ounce of his energy. He didn't know that the events of war would stick with him forever.

He didn't know that the first time he was shot at, he would cry afterward. The first time he experienced an IED, it made him question life. The time where he thought going to war was the right thing to do soon disappeared as doubt and guilt took over. Watching others like Sergeant R escape death multiple times really put his life in perspective. The times where he thought that he was invincible were no more. He was lucky to be alive, I thought. I smiled as I put the picture on top of my sea bag and went back to duty.

NUMB

BOOZE WAS SCARCE. ANY TIME WE WERE able to get our hands on any, it was like hitting the lotto. We had many rules as it was already, but the two that stood out the most were no sex and no alcohol. For a bunch of Marines, alcohol was all we needed to help cope with the rigors of each day not to mention most of us wouldn't mind the company of a beautiful girl. We had tobacco, but a nice cold beer would satisfy us more.

I was out back of the barracks one night smoking when I overheard some guys talking by the port-a-johns. I walked toward them, thinking it was Kyle or Slipknot out there enjoying a Marlboro. The closer I got, I saw that it was a couple of guys from my platoon with one of them holding a bottle in his hand. I knew it wasn't alcohol since the bottle was small and it had a white label. I heard some guys were going to the Public Exchange and buying Robitussen and Nyquil, hoping that drinking enough of it would make them drunk. I hoped it wasn't either of those items but my eyes were telling me otherwise. I wanted to walk over and stop them. They didn't need it. I was here for them. Everyone in our unit was going through their own hardship. If they wanted to talk about the stress of being out here, any of us would've listened. I was dealing with my own personal struggles being out here and talking with them would help us both through our tribulations.

But I knew that some guys didn't want to talk about their personal issues. They would rather drink than share their feelings. The cough syrup made them feel no pain. When I came home from convoys, there were times I would see empty cough syrup bottles in the trash can and strewn around the room. I shook my head, not in disgust but more in sadness that my friends were struggling to the point that codeine helped them more than a good meal or conversation.

I put out my cigarette and walked back to the barracks. I didn't say anything to them that night. I didn't try to stop them. Even though it saddened me and I felt guilt, drinking cough syrup was their way of coping. During the Vietnam War, guys were in the middle of the jungle, drinking whenever they could to help ease the pain of combat. They were getting shot day in and out. None of their buddies were stopping those who drank from doing it. No one was saying to them "You need to stop drinking. We can talk about your problems over an MRE." All the dead bodies, all the violence made drinking their only outlet.

For our unit, we were fortunate not to have lost anyone but we dealt with constant fear of our environment. We never knew when the next bomb would go off. We didn't know when a mortar was going to drop out of the sky onto us. The fear was what got us the most, not knowing when the next attack would happen. It was always a guessing game. Whenever we got our hands on alcohol, it was to deal with living in war. The times I drank out in Iraq, it made the stress all disappear. It made everything go away.

I always felt I should've said something to the guys about the cough syrup. The cough syrup was extremely harmful, especially since we were motor transport; being intoxicated behind the wheel would've put the unit at risk. But I felt for them. I was drinking liquor out in Iraq. While I was drinking, I didn't have to worry for my life. The guys didn't have to worry about their safety or shit they had going on when they drank, too. They could pass the bottle instead, hoping that the cough syrup would take effect quickly. Whether it was cough syrup or alcohol, it made the deployment easier.

LAUGH

December 2004 Operation Iraqi Freedom II Tour 1

"*I STILL HAVEN'T KILLED ANYONE. IT bothers me. I drive hundreds of miles each week and all I see on the roads are IED's and landmines. Still haven't had any close encounters like the incident at Al Quim. Being a marine means shooting. It means getting paid to kill, to wipe out the scum of the earth with my M16 rifle. I feel I'm only doing half my job the Marine Corps sent me here to do, which is drive convoys. Every day I drive, dropping supplies off at multiple Forward Operating bases around the Al Anbar province. I am doing my job successfully. I am failing at being a Marine.*

Whenever I go to the computer lab here on base to check my bank account, I see the large amount of money deposited from the

Marines. A sense of greed overcomes me and my thoughts of fail-
ure disappear. It makes me think more about money and less
about war. I think less about my safety and more about the mo-
torcycle I want to buy when I go home. It feels wrong to think
about the money. I am here to fight for freedom, for everyone back
home. For a second, I think about giving back half my paycheck
to offset my greed and guilt that I am not fulfilling my role as a
Marine. But I just end up staring at the number on the screen."

Whenever we went to Forward Operating Base Korean
Village, it was always an overnight run. It took longer traveling
there than it did coming back due to some IED hanging from a
broken light pole on the main highway, strapped underneath an
overpass or buried next to the highway. Insurgents would take
small household items, such as a washer and dryer timer, strap
them to old 155mm howitzer tank rounds or grab some landmines and bury them a couple feet in the ground. Whenever
we did find one of the hanging explosives or buried landmines,
security halts involved three hours standing on the side of the
highway, waiting for Explosive Ordinance Disposal to disarm it.

Each and every time security halts took place, some of us
talked about the possibility of snipers shooting, never letting
ourselves see it as a real threat, joking about how we could
stand in a large group and $20 bucks says we wouldn't get shot.
We had a better chance of getting blown up than we did getting
picked off by snipers. When I first got to Iraq, I was all about
being alert, looking for my moment to pull the trigger. I kept my
head on a swivel, scanning 180 degrees with wide eyes. I threw
in extra chews during security halts just to be jacked up on nicotine, fidgeting uncontrollably, and waiting for something to go
down. I waited the entire security halt. I waited for an insurgent to come out from behind a house and shoot rounds at us.
Now, I'm waiting the entire security halt, staring out distantly

at the miles of never-ending dirt and sand leaning against my truck with extra chew thrown in my mouth betting on my life.

My passenger, Corporal Slipknot, was one of the few guys I didn't feel scared to die around. He was fearless in the face of battle from the stories he told us from the initial invasion of Iraq in 2003. Most of the conversations he had with me involved how much he wanted to shoot a machine gun at a platoon of insurgents. He had a more developed killer instinct than other Marines I had ridden with. His experience and his thirst for killing made me feel safe. When Staff Sergeant chewed his and the other noncommissioned officers' asses, it was then that Slipknot turned into Corporal Slipknot, a volatile, irritable younger version of Staff Sergeant looking to chew some Marine's ass for something. But there was another side to him, a side more human and laid back. He joked like I did about security halts and all the bullshit Staff Sergeant would make us do. He was true to his word, genuine, and honest about the intricacies of war and his experiences in it. He looked out for us when Staff Sergeant wasn't breathing down his neck. He was a warrior. He liked the nature of war, the way he was able to express his emotions through shooting a machine gun. He was about the men under his supervision. He made sure we were all going home safe to our loved ones. If it meant killing to have us be safe, then in his mind that's what it took. He was the perfect guy to ride with on a day where I didn't feel like being alert and vigilant.

The convoy mounted back up after Explosive Ordinance Disposal checked out a suspicious item strapped underneath an overpass. Slipknot and I took the last drags of our cigarettes, threw them into the sand, and stepped on the gas back onto Highway 1. The wind had picked up a little bit, sweeping sand across the highway. A couple miles into driving as I lit my cigarette, a car made its way into the middle of the convoy, swerving in and out missing the front of our truck by inches.

The car made its way in front of and behind our truck, speeding up, slowing down. I didn't know what the driver was thinking, attempting to integrate within the ranks of the convoy. It did happen on a couple of convoys previously where Iraqi civilians would accidently end up in the middle of our convoys. We would simply end up waving them off the road; they responded immediately. This wasn't an accident. I sensed this car had a purpose. I stepped on the gas, slamming the pedal down until it hit the floorboard, hoping that I could outrun the car without having to wave at him and that the car's attempted integration was an accident.

The turbocharger roared as the car sped up closer and closer, every foot of highway disappearing as it came towards us. I grabbed my M-16 latched onto the door, pushed a round into the chamber, while my knee steered the truck. Slipknot, cigarette lit and calm as ever could be, had his M240 locked and loaded. He swiftly positioned the machine gun out the window, simultaneously waving his arm, hoping the car wasn't in our convoy by accident.

"Liguori, I'm shooting a fucking flare."

The car moved more rapidly, swerving around our truck from front to back. Slipknot grabbed the flare from the ammo box, removing the lid and pointed it right at the driver. The flare burst out of the canister with a slap of Slipknot's hand, bouncing off the hood of the vehicle. The driver of the car didn't see us.

I shot at the ground immediately as the driver whipped his car to the driver side of my truck. He still kept driving faster and faster, toying with us as if we were hungry caged lions. I took a couple more seconds to aim and pulled the trigger several times, hitting the car across the bumper grill. He turned sharply to the other side of our truck in response before I could empty out the rest of the cartridge.

I had never seen anyone look more excited, so incredibly thrilled to shoot someone than Slipknot. His eyes grew large like a wolf circling a helpless deer, eager and intent. His jaw clenched as he gripped the trigger. Everything about him was precise, full of tactical positioning for his kill. A short moment of silence filled the cab after he racked some rounds into the chamber. He let out a war cry as rounds exited from his machine gun. Thud, thud, thud. Rounds struck the engine viciously the longer Slipknot held the trigger. Rounds more widespread across the vehicle than mine were. I watched Slipknot with slight worry. Earlier on the security halt, he was joking, smoking a cigarette, talking music with me. Now, he was a killing machine with no off switch.

I waited for the delay, that the driver would detonate a bomb strapped to his car. For the explosion. The shock waves. Death...nothing. The car pulled to the side of the road, the driver emphatically waving his arms at us. I kept driving, onward into the sunset where Korean Village lay vaguely in the distance, the car smoking in my side mirrors.

I kept cursing myself how horrible of a shot I must be to miss a moving vehicle yards away from my window. I wish I would've hit the driver with my rounds. I didn't need evidence to know he was a threat. I saw the dark details of his face, the sudden openings of his eyes as if he were ready to die. He had driven into our convoy. It was enough to justify my actions. Really, I wanted him to die so I know that my combat training worked. I wanted to feel I would leave Iraq accomplished, another insurgent dead. But I almost died again without killing. I ended up laughing.

Slipknot nudged me in the shoulder with his elbow as he opened the cover tray of the machine gun and cleaned out the shell casings.

"Fucking dumbass haji." He said. "You think he would know that if you see big ass green trucks with guns on them, you fucking stay away."

Slipknot's hands quietly shook, while his face displayed nothing but stability. He started to laugh a little as well, more at the driver's moronic behavior than at the fear of almost dying. Maybe it was both.

"Yeah, I know, man. I couldn't believe that shit. What the fuck was that asshole thinking?" I hesitantly responded. I lit up a cigarette to calm my nervousness. Slipknot asked for one, he grabbed it before I could even answer. He lit up and we smoked a whole pack in the next hour.

SMOKES

January 2005 Operation Iraqi Freedom II Tour I

"*THE FEAR OF WAR AND DEATH ARE MINIMAL. I don't feel scared about my death. I think about it so much that to die out in this place feels like my destiny. There was still a piece of me, the human piece that feared the unknown. There are times when the emotions and anxiety of the unknown surface. I have to keep it bottled up. There is no room for it out in Iraq. It could get me killed if I broke down during a firefight. It could make me a liability if my unit saw any sign of emotional instability. They wouldn't be able to trust that I could fire back when needed. I haven't been able to compile my own thoughts and feelings without being tired. The nicotine from each cigarette makes me feel invincible. It makes me feel I could work longer and stay awake on the convoys during the tumultuous journeys to Korean Village. It makes me feel unemotional, cold inside."*

We were going to Hit, a small base down the road from Al Asad. I called Hit "The Surprise" since I never knew what kind of event would happen there. Anything from a car bombing at the front gate or an angry mob of one hundred plus people protesting of the U.S. could happen. Hit was maybe half the size of the bases that we usually traveled to. Two buildings housed the entire infantry company. It had everything inside, including their sleeping quarters. They had a makeshift Internet and phone call station set up in a room no bigger than a high school classroom. Eating in the Chow Hall felt like being crammed inside a can of sardines. The small size of the camp definitely affected morale.

We had all these luxuries. We had a huge internet and phone center. The Al Asad Chow Hall had been renovated and was about the size of a football field. We had probably the best food in Iraq and in addition we had access to an abundance of DVDs. The infantry company at Hit had nothing in comparison to my life out at Al Asad. They dealt with violence regularly on their patrols and took daily mortar attacks. All they had was an abundance of ammunition, a shipment of tobacco to hold them over till we brought more the following week, and each other.

Each time I went to Hit, I looked forward to living like the infantry. I wanted to consider myself a "grunt," a term used for guys whose military occupational specialty was infantry even if it was for only one night. Maybe go out on a patrol, search for insurgents, pop off some rounds from my rifle, and come back to base. Have a nice cup of coffee. It sounded great. It was new and exciting to stay here. It also gave me a better chance to achieve my first kill.

I off loaded my pallet at the ammo lot as fast as I could, full of excitement and anticipation about what conflict might happen during my stay. I wanted to be ready if anything was going to happen. The thought, of shooting and finally being in a firefight was thrilling. I brought my sleeping gear to a small room in one of the two buildings with the others and grabbed my rifle, helmet, and jacket, eager to volunteer for a patrol with the infantry unit.

I waited near the company office, ammo magazine gripped in my left hand. I waited and waited, hoping some patrol leader would see my willingness and take me along with his unit.

"Is there a reason why you're standing outside like you're going on patrol?" One of the guys from our convoy said, shaking his head laughing at me.

I didn't know what was so funny. I was here to help the infantry company go on patrol, give them an extra man if needed. I was positive they had some guys who needed a break from patrols.

"No, not really. Just felt like standing out here, enjoy the sun a bit." I was thoroughly embarrassed. The guy knew I was full of shit and I looked like a fool standing outside the company office ready for combat when I knew damn well there was no combat to be had. He turned his head, not saying anything to me as he walked back into the small room, still chuckling out loud. I did look a little ridiculous, I thought. I glanced over my gear, making sure every strap and pouch was secure. I walked back toward our sleeping area, turning my head that maybe someone would come out and pick me. No one ever did as I slowly took my gear off, hanging my vest and helmet over my arm while I opened the door.

The guys and some drivers from the civilian truck company Kellogg Brown and Root (KBR) started a game of spades. Spades was great. Not only did it bring some interest to our days, it gave us an opportunity to bond. We got to know each other very well. We developed a bond strong enough to rival that of a sibling relationship. Spider, Mud Dog, Mississippi, the KBR guys, were some of the most loyal people I have ever met. They all had beards, wore American flag bandanas wrapped around some part of their body and sported well-groomed mullets. They looked like guys who were still fighting the civil war and Lynyrd Skynyrd wasn't just a band to them but it rather embodied the lifestyle of the American way.

I felt my confidence slowly deteriorate since I lost my fifth straight hand. A cigarette sounded just about right to help ease the sting of my defeat. I walked outside to my truck, kicking my frustrations into the loose gravel with every step. One of the guys in my unit, Husky, was already smoking outside. He paced back and forth, kicking up the same gravel carelessly as he murmured words to himself underneath his breath.

Husky was more frustrated than he was pissed. I think losing just really got to him. He was mostly a pretty even-keeled guy but had a competitive side that was equipped with a short fuse. The few times I was around him whenever he lost playing Xbox or a game of cards, he would expel his temper through a slew of vulgar words. It would make me laugh, hearing him scream "shit" and "fuck," combined together at the top of his lungs.

Husky and I sat there on our smoke break and nodded in recognition that we had both had our asses handed to us by the KBR guys. A bunch of Southern Truckers kicked our ass at the game Spades that we had been playing every day since we landed in country. We were upset. We had both figured that we were experts at the game since we played it so damn much. We were both so pissed off.

The previous times at Hit, I could usually hear the four-cylinder engines of cars driving past the base. I could hear the forklift beeping in the distance as it loaded and off-loaded pallets. I could watch the wind gently pick up the sand. I pulled a Marlboro No.27 pack right out of my breast pocket, fumbling with the ends to make sure that I didn't accidently smoke the filter. My lighter had just enough fluid left. Faithfully, I shook it, hoping I could squeeze out one more flame.

I got enough of a spark to lighting the end of my cigarette as I shielded it from the wind. There was a moment of silence then. Sand started to jump up, passing by us. The wind blew harder, hurling the bottom of my shirt upward and almost blowing the soft cover off my head. My stomach became tangled in knots. The hairs on the back of neck stood at attention.

I felt my whole body freeze. It never had done that before, not even during the times when I had seen IED's or watched explosions on previous convoys. Husky was in the same state as I was, the only movement between us was the smoke drifting upward into the air from our cigarettes. When the wind was at its strongest, when the sand was moving with force, and when the silence grew the most deafening, it suddenly stopped.

Mortars rained around us, rippling massively across the ground. I ran as fast as I could back inside the nearest building. I didn't look back to see if Husky was right behind me. I just hoped he was.

Husky appeared out of the corner of my eye, pumping his arms with all his might. He ran faster than all of the times that we had physical training runs at Camp Pendleton. His boots hit the ground, pounding with every step. I was sure that both of us would make it inside without a scratch. He gained enough ground on me that I was sure he was behind me underneath the doorway. We were both going to be okay.

I reached for the door only to realize that Husky wasn't next to me. I turned my head back towards the trucks to see Husky sprint back out into the chaos, his shirt half-unbuttoned, hat hanging on the back of his head, bootlaces untied as he braved the metal rain storm. I wanted to rush out there to grab him. I had to save him. I didn't want his family to have to hear that he died for a three-dollar pack of smokes if a mortar hit him. He was part of our unit, a brother in arms. I couldn't leave a man behind. But the distance between us had grown. He was already out in the open.

His eyes were wide with fear. Husky grabbed his smokes off the truck's bumper, strangling the pack with a Kung Fu grip. The impact of a mortar dictated his next step as he tripped, lost his footing and almost fell to the ground. He regained his traction and sprinted back to the building. Smokes in hand, he jogged the last few feet until he was underneath the doorway. I rushed him in, slammed the door, and stood in silence until the alarm sounded that the mortars crashing down upon us had stopped.

The rest of the guys were in awe of Husky braving the mortar attack. They asked him if he was okay, if he got hit at all. Of course, just like any Marine would, he said he was fine, a little smile stretched across his face. When he made eye contact with me, he didn't say a word. He looked at the ground, quickly walking by, hoping I wouldn't say anything to him. He knew I thought he was a fucking idiot.

The guys and I proceeded outside toward the trucks to smoke once again, waiting to hear Husky's account of the mortar attack. We gathered around, passing lighters and cigarettes between us. Husky stood across from me in the small circle, going about his business as usual. Mortars were something we got used to out in Iraq. Finding shelter during thirty seconds of a torrential downpour of metal was normal. But Husky running out in the middle of it for a pack of smokes wasn't.

Husk opened the top of his cigarette pack while holding his lighter in his clenched fist. He smiled out of the corner of his mouth as I watched him and immediately became infuriated.

"You know you could've died, dumbass!"

Husky attempted to straighten his shirt out, tightening his belt and even swiping at some dirt on his trousers. He pulled a cigarette out of the crinkled pack. He chuckled, the sound ringing out through his yellow-stained teeth and his well-trimmed mustache. He got a little louder, the only thing punctuating his mirth were his grimacing looks of disbelief. He looked up at me slowly, lifting the cigarette eye-level towards me.

"Dude, all that for a broken cigarette."

SODA BOP

JOSH HAD COME BACK TO AL-TAQUDDUM earlier than expected from his Al Quim convoy. He didn't even bother to knock at my door, just barged in, dropped his gear, and slapped his hand on my shoulder. He was smiling from ear to ear, pacing quickly, with every step ready to explode with today's events.

"Mike, you aren't going to believe what I saw today. Funniest shit I have ever seen in my life."

I looked at him with a deer in the headlights look. Josh was not one to get this excited about something unless it made him laugh hysterically or it was very important. It had to be good.

"Well, Josh, what's this great story you have to tell me? Is it really the funniest shit you've ever seen?"

He paused for a second, and then went to grab the chair, pulling it beneath him. He adjusted his position for a slight second, making sure he was completely comfortable before getting into his expedition. He started off by telling me how much Al Quim sucked as I laughed in agreement with him.

Josh rode in the front seat. As predicted, he brought snack foods, a portable DVD player, and a brain full of quips and short stories that involved the best humor possible. Those were essential items to him. He saw this convoy as more of tourist attraction rather than being preoccupied with its danger. He didn't see anything out of the ordinary on the way to Al Quim, and that the kids were a little volatile. He told me about all the sounds, the fear, and the kids that I was so familiar with and how they had thrown rocks, yelled, and screamed in Arabic at the convoy.

"It was weird, Mike. I remember you telling me about the time they attacked you. I didn't think they were going to throw grenades or any of that stuff when I passed through. But it was just weird because they were waving at us, a lot of them now that I think of it."

I couldn't believe that all the times I had told my story about the kids from Al Quim to others, how brutal and ruthless they were; it turned out now they seemed to like us.

As Josh and his convoy arrived at Al Quim, the off load process began. Josh wary of his new surroundings stepped into the newly built Chow Hall. He made a valiant attempt at trying to fit every morsel of the hot meal into his mouth before they had to turn around and drive back to Al-Taquddum.

During dinner, Josh asked his driver, Matt, if they were going the same way back to camp as they had come here. Matt closed his mouth full of food, looked at Josh in bewilderment.

"Yeah, why wouldn't we? You think we are going to blaze our own fucking trail back to Al Taquddum."

Josh didn't respond to him. He didn't know how they were going to get back. Instead of asking more questions to Matt about the convoy, Josh kept silent and decided to fill his cargo pant pockets full of candy, stuffing every inch until wrappers were poking over the top seam of his cargo pockets. His big heart couldn't resist the kids I despised so much. He saw how run down the village was, the roads filled with IED potholes and piles of garbage spread throughout. He mentioned the kids' faces and clothes, how sand-stained they were. Josh couldn't stand to see kids living in poverty. He hoped some candy might bring them happiness.

After chow, the convoy lined up in formation for accountability and got back in the trucks to make their way back to camp. They passed the cement factory on the left and took a right turn into the village. Josh's truck made its entrance into the village. He dug into his pockets and began the candy shower. The candy flew from his hand, landing in every direction as kids rushed full speed to get their hands on a piece. They jumped for joy, screaming in delight full of cheer, some even waving back at him to signal thank you.

At that moment, the convoy decided to do a security halt, right in the middle of the fucking village. At that instant, Josh had run out of candy. He knew it was just his luck that he was going to have to get out and stand with his rifle, the children surrounding him separated only by a chain link fence.

"I swear I thought they were going to jump me, Mike. They looked like a pack of rabid dogs. I was hoping they would maybe leave me alone."

The kids kept getting louder, barking at him for more candy and food. Josh tried to explain to them that he didn't have any food left, but the kids refused to take his apology, shaking the fence hard for Skittles.

One child particular stood out to Josh during the security halt.

"He kept rubbing his stomach in circles at me. I knew he wanted candy but it was like he could care less about my explanation." Josh said.

Josh threw his hands in the air as if he didn't know what else he was supposed to do in that situation. Even I, the seasoned vet of Al Quim, couldn't tell him what I would've done differently in the situation.

"Mista, Mista. Hungry need food, need food." The kid kept motioning to Josh with his small hands, repeatedly making circular motions with his small hands.

The small child reached through the chain link fence, pointing at Josh's truck. Josh's side of the truck was filled with enough supplies to last a weekend camping trip, but the kid was pointing at one of Josh's most prized possessions; a 12-pack of Pepsi. Josh would have given anything to that kid, even the shirt off his back. But the Pepsi was Josh's most valuable possession.

Josh took a sip of Gatorade, wiping his mouth with his sleeve as he continued to tell his tale.

"I would've given something to the kid. But kid pointed right at my Pepsi. At first I was like, 'Yeah, fucking right, I'm giving you Pepsi.'"

I paused for a moment, doing a quick analysis of Josh's statement. I knew the guy too well. He was too good of a friend, let alone too good of a person. There was no way he didn't cave in to the kid.

"You gave him the Pepsi, didn't you?"

Josh started to laugh. He couldn't bullshit me. He never answered my question directly, avoiding it with a "Just let me finish the story."

Josh pointed along with the kid at the Pepsi that sat next to his seat on the center console. The kid's arms waved in excitement. Josh walked backwards, scanning left to right. He needed to make sure he kept some sort of vigilance and awareness during the security halt. He grabbed the handle on the side of the truck, hoisted himself into the cab, grabbed a Pepsi from his 12-pack, and walked back into the vicinity of the fence with an outstretched arm.

The kid's eyes widened with joy as Josh stepped closer to the fence. Josh saw that the fence's holes were not big enough to pass the soda through. So like any other American guy would in that situation, Josh figured that if he couldn't push it through, why not throw it over the fence? He thought the kid must know how to play catch. He couldn't have been younger than seven years old. He figured the young boy had to have tossed a ball with his father like Josh had done with his dad during Josh's childhood.

Josh spoke slowly, mouthing to the kid, "I'm going to throw this to you." The fence was about eight feet high and according to Josh, the Pepsi would land perfectly in the kid's arms. Acknowledging that the kid understood Josh, the kid nodded his head, raised his hands up to the sky, wide enough to embrace the Pepsi with love and affection. Josh made eye contact with this kid, nodding his head in rhythm as he counted to three, releasing the Pepsi from his hand. The can soared into a high arc, high enough to clear the barbwire at the pinnacle.

The kid watched the can as it flew swiftly over the fence, rapidly descending into his awaiting arms. The other kids looked on as the can picked up speed. They stood in amazement; their faces full of hope that their friend would safely catch the Pepsi. There was a moment, Josh said, when the kids all rushed down the fence that he realized we are in Iraq, in the middle of a village. The American tradition of playing catch with your dad didn't exist here.

The boy's eyes were lifted to the sky, his hands lifted up. His outstretched arms couldn't come together fast enough; he clamored to catch the can as it whizzed through his hands. It hit him square in the face. The thump and impact of the collision were unified as the boy flew back, stunned by the full force of the can as it knocked him to the ground. There was a brief silence; Josh paused to see how the crowd of kids would react to his botched attempt to give the kid a soda.

"So, wait. You're telling me you knocked a kid out with a Pepsi can?" I asked.

Josh replied. "Mike, I swear. I couldn't believe I did it. I figured he knew how to play catch. I mean, I didn't throw it that hard at him. It was a nice toss."

Josh was so persistent about the innocence of his intent. But no matter how convincing he tried to be, Josh's laughter told a different story. Pepsi sprayed all over the ground, dampening the boy's clothes. The fizz alerted the other kids that the Pepsi was fair game. They rushed over, wrestling one another over the can as the kid cried out in pain. Josh had never seen kids biting, pushing, and tearing at one another that way before. The juvenile mob grew, pushing and kicking the kid aside. They created a massive dog pile, jumping on each other, scrapping for the opened can.

At that moment, the security halt ended as the massive group of kids continued to grow more violent. Josh ran to his truck as fast as he could, laughing and gasping for air at the mess he had made. He peered out of the passenger side window, watching the wrestling match while he buckled his seat belt.

Josh couldn't keep his laughter inside. "Matt started cracking up, too, when we were driving back. I mean, the whole entire way back from Al Quim, we were laughing."

After the story, I couldn't help but laugh too. Josh had managed to do more damage to the kids of Al Quim with a Pepsi can than I did with my rifle.

MISFIRE

I WAS ON MOTOR POOL GUARD DUTY IN THE middle of winter. Duties rotated every couple weeks so guys could get a break from the monotony of the convoys. It was nice being able to relax, be on some sort of schedule, and get adequate hours of sleep. We got to eat at the Chow Hall every day, sleep in quiet without farting, or hearing some guy talk in his sleep across the room.

After a while, it became one of the worst duties. Usually after a week on motor pool guard duty, guys were getting restless, anxious to get back on the road. The winter months made everything more difficult. The air was crisper, but the temperature drop between day to night was drastic. It would be 70 degrees during the day, which is cool for Iraq, then drop down into the 40s at night fall. At least driving on a convoy, we had the chance to get assigned a truck with a heater, but then again you might get stuck up on the gun turret.

I sat around the fire, slouching in patio chairs with my rifle dangling between my legs. The other guard and I smoked a whole pack or would go through whole cans of dip in one sitting, sometimes both to make sure we stayed awake all night. Once in a while, a pack of wild dogs ran by one another like a game of tag. The dogs were never threatening, but we were ordered to shoot them if they came close to us due to the fear of rabies or disease they might carry. I never intentionally sought the dogs out to try to kill them for my own cheap thrills, but there were times I wished they would come close enough. I needed to let out some frustration. The irritability and ever-growing anger from being in Iraq weighed on me so heavy that squeezing the trigger at anything would make it go away.

On one of these typical nights, my platoon's convoy had come back from a long journey. It was always good to see everyone come back safe in one piece. I was overjoyed to see that there was no damage to the trucks and the only thing suffered from the convoys were fatigue. Everyone could sleep in their racks without having to worry about dying for a couple of hours.

Staff Sergeant was a different story when it came to feeling any sort of joy. I was glad he was back but I hoped in any confrontation I could have with him, he would be too tired to find something wrong and not chew my ass. He was still motivated as hell, striding around like a drill instructor at the recruit depot in San Diego.

Staff Sergeant made his way toward me, striking the deck with enough force to start an earthquake.

"Liguori, why didn't you frickin' ask who was approaching the gate?"

"I didn't think I needed to, Staff Sergeant. I knew it was you."

"Devil Dog, I don't care if you knew it was me, you frickin' ask who is approaching the goddamn gate!"

Staff Sergeant's wrinkled eyes looked at me hard, frustrated with my answer. I knew he wanted to say something else that would push me to inch one step closer, reach my fist back, and sock him square in his face. But he just walked away before I could say or do anything I would regret.

That was his way of asserting power with me. He would say something to me, something that would hit the very core of me, knowing it would piss me off, and wait for a reaction. Before I had a chance to tactfully stand my ground, he'd turn his back right before I could get a word out. He would march on his way to find more people to dominate. I wished every day that he would get a taste of his own medicine.

When convoys came into any base, weapons were to be "cleared" at the entrance of the base gate, meaning all rounds from every firearm must be confirmed empty by a noncommissioned officer or a higher rank officer. Of course, Staff Sergeant enjoyed this type of responsibility and he headed over to where the trucks were parked to make sure the weapons were clear. He loved being in charge. It was the drill instructor in him. Nothing made Staff Sergeant happier than to chew out someone of a lower rank when they made a mistake.

One by one, Staff Sergeant climbed up and down each truck with a machine gun and scanned the weapons, looking for the one gun that wasn't cleared. Staff Sergeant made his way to the top of a seven-ton truck that had a .50 caliber machine gun on the turret. He scaled up the truck with intensity and speed. With each movement, he covered the short distance between himself and the machine gun turret. As he reached the top, he straddled the gun, opening the cover with a strong grip. His eyes were wide as his hands squeezed the life out of every piece of metal.

He proceeded through his memorized gun safety checklist, pulling back the charging handle of the gun to verify there were no rounds in the chamber. He peered inside, using the small spotlight of his flashlight, searching every corner with his intense gaze. The charging handle suddenly slipped, sliding forward out of his grasp. A round exploded out of the barrel.

The round came out fast, traveling feet above me for a split second, leaving a trail of red light behind, and disappeared into the horizon, swallowed by the dark blue sky.

I choked as I inhaled my Newport. My lungs felt they were going to pop out of my chest. I was shocked my wish had been answered. The misfire in the motor pool was a mistake that would not go unnoticed. Staff Sergeant was sure to be screwed beyond all belief.

Staff Sergeant was embarrassed, stunned that his typical attention to the finest detail had led to a discharged round inside the confines of Al Asad. He was disgusted at himself. He wanted to thrash himself as he did recruits on the drill field, do thousands of push-ups until the pain in his arms made him puke. He had failed to stay perfect in front of his platoon for the first time in his career. For that small moment, he was one of us. He was vulnerable, alone, and human.

The awkward silence of everyone staring at him, wondering if what they had just heard was a round fired was terrifying to Staff Sergeant. Staff Sergeant was pissed, turning red with anger, wishing he could turn on someone to chew them out. His veins bulged in his face. His hands moved violently, grasping the handles as he scrambled down the truck, looking for the driver and the gunner.

The driver and gunner of the truck just kept looking at it in shock. They knew Staff Sergeant was going to lose his mind if he found out it was both of them. I watched them whisper to each other, looking around hoping to find an escape route to avoid Staff Sergeant's wrath. I was still bewildered by the fact that the round had gone off feet above my head and hadn't hit me.

As everyone attempted to get back to cleaning out the trucks, the two guys made their way close to the motor pool fence, hoping the darkness of the area would conceal them. Just like prisoners caught trying to escape jail, the huge spotlight at the entrance of the motor pool shone on them as Staff Sergeant glanced the same time they had almost made their exit.

"Hey, you two get over here right now, devil dogs!" Staff Sergeant screamed at the top of his lungs.

The two guys stopped in their tracks, glancing at each other knowing they were in deep shit. Simultaneously, they turned around and rapidly sprinted over to Staff Sergeant's position.

"What the fuck were you thinking, devil dogs? How in the hell are you going to let a gun become unclear in my motor pool. Do you realize how many fucking Marines you could've killed? Well, do you?!"

Staff Sergeant took a firm position, making sure he towered as much as he could with his 5'9" frame over the 6 foot tall junior Marines. He tilted his hat back a bit on his head, attempting to restrain himself from choking the guys.

"Nothing, Staff Sergeant," they replied in unison

'Nothing, what the hell does nothing mean? I didn't ask you what you were doing."

Staff Sergeant stared at them hard, attempting to pierce their frightened faces. He wiped the sweat off his brow and repositioned his hat tightly two inches above his nose, enough to see his eyes peer beneath the hat brim as a drill instructor would do to signal to recruits he was ready to thrash them.

"You gotta be shitting me." Staff Sergeant said. "That's the best damn answer you can come up with? Of course you dumb fucks would say 'nothing.' Both of you let a round go off and almost killed Marines."

"Yes, Staff Sergeant."

It was all the junior marines could say. In the Marines, everything is checked twice to make sure no mistakes are made. The gunner had failed to clear his weapon properly. His driver failed to check the weapon twice. They had screwed up but the responsibility fell on Staff Sergeant. He knew that the misfired round could jeopardize his career, especially if the round killed marines.

"I'll deal with you two later. Clean out your truck and wait for me back at the barracks." Staff Sergeant waved his hand dismissingly as the two marines ran over to their truck and finished cleaning.

Twenty minutes later, a Humvee pulled up with three men sitting in the seats, straddling the roll cage of the open top vehicle. I couldn't see their faces because of insufficient lighting, but the glare of their insignia was bright enough that no light was needed. I knew that officers had arrived on deck and were making their way towards the gate.

One of the Officers signaled me to approach him. The closer I walked toward him, the better I could see his face and the shiny bars on his collar.

"Marine, what is your name?" he asked me.

"Lance Corporal Liguori, sir."

"Who is in charge tonight?"

My mind sped through the list of answers I could give the officer. I could've told him I had no idea but I would be lying. I didn't like Staff Sergeant though. I could've sought out complete revenge for the punch Staff Sergeant threw during a football game last month or how demeaning he was to me. I wanted him to be paid back for how he treated all of us as if we were recruits. No matter how strong my feelings of dislike were towards him, I couldn't say his name. There was something my conscience kept bringing to the surface about revenge. Although he talked down to us and treated me with disrespect, I couldn't bring myself to that level when the officer asked for his name. I don't know why, it just didn't feel satisfying to pay him back.

"I think he's over there somewhere, sir." I ended up pointing somewhere random in the motor pool near the other guys in my unit.

All three of them walked into the motor pool, strides in step with one another. They searched and asked some of the others where Staff Sergeant might be. They called for him, as Staff Sergeant walked over towards where his name was called. He was surrounded by three officers, ready to lay into him with everything they had. They circled him, tilting their hats forward near their noses as they were ready to scream and curse. Staff Sergeant welcomed the challenge, his hands interlocked behind his back. He turned his head to each question the officers asked. I could hear them, scolding Staff Sergeant with pointed fingers and spit flying out of their mouths.

"So Staff Sergeant, you care to explain how the fuck a round ends up on my side of the camp, ten feet above three marines who were smoking outside?"

I watched Staff Sergeant stand respectfully and submissively as the officers cornered his ego and beat it to a pulp. He was outnumbered, outmanned, and outranked. He had no response for their questions, his head up and down in compliance with whatever they said. Standing in the presence of three officers while they gnawed and bit at every part of his broken self, he was shamed, embarrassed and in denial. His head drifted lower and lower to the side, then down.

The ass-chewing lasted only a minute or two, but it was long enough to bring a bit of a smile to my face. He now knew how I felt whenever he disrespected me with his drill instructor talk. Even though I didn't feel right giving his name up to the officers, a part of me was glad that there was the possibility the misfire would inspire in him some sort of revelation. I hoped that he would've told me that he was sorry for punching me in the face earlier in the deployment and that he would do whatever he could to make our situation better by working on talking to me like a man and not a kid. I hoped the officers' ass-chewing brought him back to his day as a recruit where he had no power, no rank, no responsibility. I wished it would've reminded him about what it was like to be human, to be at fault for mistakes, and to feel humility.

As the officers marched back to their Humvee, all of these hopes flashed in my mind. Staff Sergeant had taken his ass-chewing like a man, wiped his brow with the back of his hand, turned and screamed at us until we got into formation.

MORNING FIREWORKS

THE AIR NEVER SMELLED SO WONDERFUL. I almost felt like I was camping in the mountains, breathing in fresh air and enjoying the scenery, except there was no scenery to enjoy. I had been residing in a base surrounded by sand dunes for the past seven months. Today was different. There were no more convoys. There were no more sleepless nights. In two days, I would land in Kuwait, out of harm's way and out of all this insanity. Everything I had dreaded, all the hypervigilance and miles of driving were going to disappear. All of the IEDs scattered among the roads, the constant mental fatigue would no longer be a hazard for me. The smokeless tobacco in my mouth tasted sweeter, the sun in the sky seemed brighter. It was all good.

During my tour, I always went to breakfast with someone. Usually Kevin accompanied me but I decided I would eat by myself today. I needed to reflect on my thoughts, how I had been able to survive all these months. Even though today brought me one day closer to my departure back to California, I still felt like the end of my life was close. I could feel it so intensely during my walk to the Chow Hall. I thought of when I would die, instead of if I would die. I waited for a mortar to drop out of the sky and hit me square in the chest. I didn't know how to shut off my senses. The little bit of me that was still intact believed that home would make all the fears disappear. The combat-hardened side hoped a cup of Folgers drip coffee and a plate full of powdered eggs would get me through another day.

After I finished at the Chow Hall, I made my way back to Tent City, where our unit waited for our flight. I crossed paths with this guy Otto on my way back from the Chow Hall. Otto was always angry. He shared the same patriotism I exuded. He joined to fight the war as I did. We were previously stationed in Okinawa together, back when every crease in his pants, the way his cover sat, and his use of military lingo showed his deep passion for the Corps. Our conversations had consisted of our preference of machine gun if we were to be shot at or if we were hand to hand with the enemy, what combo or move we would use to kill them.

That was before the war. That was before we saw bombs explode, the depths of hatred other countries had for America, and the simply unpredictable boredom that we dealt with every day in the Sandbox. We prayed hard that our chance would come to fight, anticipating all the tactics and training we would get to use out in war. Otto had a little bit of a skip in his step, his boots happily throwing dirt in the air like confetti with every step. As we made eye contact with each other, he smiled at me, revealing his signature snaggletooth in his top teeth. Everything we ever discussed about war was nothing we imagined it to be. We were both excited to get out of here. There was no need to talk to him about fighting anymore. Al I had to do was just smile back at him.

The wind, blowing gently against my face on the walk back, abruptly stopped. The familiar noises of construction equipment around base and the jets at the airfield had stopped. The sand that ran across the top of my boots had stopped in place. This was all too familiar to me, the same awkward moments of silence I felt throughout my tour. It felt like Hit and Al Quim all over again.

A slight high-pitched whistle broke into the silence. It grew with each second. My heart stopped. I felt sweat dripping down my face, and my hands shook and twitched. My feet felt as if they were stuck in blocks of concrete. A round hit the dirt, impacting just meters away from me. The alarm sounded as my heart kicked back in. My arms pumped furiously as I grasped my rifle slung over my back, spilling cigarettes everywhere as I sprinted towards the nearest building.

I made my way, panting and sweating, into the barracks we had just moved out of days ago. The attack lasted seconds but seemed like minutes. I watched the last seconds of the attack out one of the windows. I hoped that none of the mortars had hit Tent City. Our unit had not lost anyone and I didn't want this mortar attack days before we left to kill anyone.

The base sounded the "all clear alarm." I walked outside as I heard the familiar noises of the runway and trucks start back up. I took a couple of steps towards Tent City. The sun was still bright. There were no clouds in the sky. It could still be a great day despite the mortars. I knew Iraq wasn't going to let me leave without putting up a fight. We had battled for seven months straight. With every mortar, IED, and mile, Iraq was going down swinging. I wasn't home free yet. It was going to make sure I knew that.

THE SANDBOX

Unexpectedly, a rocket came from out of nowhere, making a straight line for the main fuel station across the road from us. The rocket exploded into the ground of the fuel station, causing black smoke to rise from its ashes and flames to follow thereafter. I watched it move in slow motion across the desert sky. The smell of fuel burning covered most of the base.

It was the biggest fire I had ever seen. Fire trucks and ambulances surrounded it for the next three days, pouring gallons of water and dumping piles of sand hoping to extinguish the massive flame. The average person would keep a safe distance away from an explosion and fire like that. Marines, of course, are not average people. We seek danger, are enamored with explosions and weaponry. We live to see destruction. The Marines of Tent City poured out, rushing as close as they could to the fire, disposable cameras in hand, as they began to do their best impression of the paparazzi. Clicks of the wheel and flashes from the small bulbs of their cameras went off as if a famous celebrity graced the camp with their presence. There were rumors that some Marines from the other units had bought some marshmallows from the Public Exchange and made S'mores with the fuel fire. Instead of running for cover, Marines were running toward the explosion.

Days later, I got on a C130 cargo plane. I locked myself into my seat, cargo straps bound to me tight, looking one last time at the mysterious, unpredictable Iraq that had been my home. I thought about how courageous our unit was, how fear never really struck us. We stuck together and when I thought about how scared I was the entire tour, there was always someone there for me or with me who knew what I was going through. Because of the kids in the village to the mortar attacks, I knew that I wasn't ever going to be the same person I once was.

As I looked around the cabin of the plane, I saw that I wasn't alone. These men and women whom I fought with understood the fear. They knew that this place nicknamed "The Sandbox" was full of surprises. The persons they once were no longer existed. War had changed all of us.

MARINE

HIS SILENT YEARS WERE MADE UP OF DAYS full of ongoing internal battles where he longed to express how much shit he went through as a young man. War molded him into a tin man with no heart. The coldness of hatred filled his heart. Feelings of aggression and violence disconnect him from society. The Marines became his way of life. He prayed for war. He hoped for the chance to use his new-found hand-to-hand combat skills to squeeze the life out of every insurgent he encounters during his tours to the Middle East.

The moment the young marine touched down in combat, he became nervous. He felt his blood pump throughout his hands as they slightly throb from his increased heart rate. He sweats, holding his rifle in the front of his body, every pound of his pack weighing his shoulders down as he tightened the straps to lift it higher.

He had waited to see this moment, which he consistently replayed in his mind to decide how he was going to react when the rounds flew. He had been told by everyone who served during the 2003 invasion that war was nothing compared to what the movies had played it to be. War consisted of long periods of hurry up and wait, and the times he waited were the times that he begged for something to happen to break the continuous boredom. He waited for his chance to prove his worth as a man. He waited to reveal his true self to his fellow Marines so he could prove to them that war is something he is willing to bleed for. He wanted to see the combat that he was told about. He wanted to be part of history, part of the legacy where Marines face death, rejoice in combat, and triumph in undaunted courage.

As soon as the first rounds hit, he quickly experienced every human emotion, mixed with an adrenaline rush so high, that this moment, where he saw explosions, gunfire, and anger surrounding him, becomes his new drug. Innocence left his soul, slowly departed from his mind, and took away all he knew; all the things his parents told him were right to do. He soon felt the rush from the bullets and their unparalleled strength and discovered his uncanny ability to shoot while being shot at. He would never be the same.

The days lasted longer but became more comfortable and predictable for him. There weren't any secrets that the insurgents were hiding, he knew every bomb and how it was made, how the insurgents mortar him and his brothers during the long periods where the paved road was nothing but mundane.

He may have realized he asked for more than what he really wanted, but he never complained. He never says the word "quit" or "I can't do this." He stuck it out. He stayed in the war, stayed with his brothers and never said a word. The young Marine lies awake at night, whispering his silent prayers that the pain and horrors of what they've seen would go on just so he could keep doing his job.

He longed to acquire knowledge of the enemy's new tactics, not to increase his skills in warfare, but to know as much as he could of the unknown. He kept himself alert by wondering how many times a mortar would drop from the sky. The chaos of war becomes his second home. He continued to serve. He continued to do another tour. It meant something to him, fighting for everyone else back home. He fought and fought, expecting to be tired, expecting to expect his own death. Without notice or rationale, he becomes the war.

Back in the States, war was on the forefront of his mind. He thought about it every day. He never left. He remembered names of his fellow Marines, the endless number of guns, and the times with his fellow service members. It all became second nature to him, the names of those with whom he shared this rush of adrenaline.

Seclusion became their only escape and soon enough, they were lost in a sandbox that grabbed tightly to their limbs and begins to slowly drag them down until their last gasp for air and fighting chance to be human was engulfed by the perils of combat.

Life lost its appeal and became uncharted waters. The unknown territory in his life started to become scary. He was more comfortable being shot at. He was more peaceful when there were rounds coming at him and he slept on the top of his truck in the middle of the desert. Sleeping in the comfort of his bed became a hot bed for nightmares. He had them repeatedly, each detail etched in his mind. He lost each waking day to memories of the war. He second-guessed his choice to get out of the service. He thought how easy it was to be fed and to be told what to do all the time. He thought perhaps reenlistment didn't sound too bad. War sounded better than the unpredictability of daily life in society. Going back to combat seemed like a good idea.

PTSD and Life Afterwards

HOME

ILANDED BACK HOME AFTER MY SECOND deployment in 2006. It was a sunny day at Camp Pendleton. It felt great to be on American soil after a twenty-plus hour trip from the Middle East. All of our families and friends were waiting and smiling as the bus pulled on the parade deck. I never seen so many people happy at once, especially the guys on the bus. Their faces were pressed against the window, looking for their families. It was a joyous time for everyone celebrating our return.

The bus came to a halt as guys pushed to make their way down the steps of the bus. I didn't bother to rush at all. I knew I was going to be able to see my family but there was no need for me to knock people over. The line died down a bit and when I made my way down the steps, I saw my mom and brother waiting patiently for me to step off the bus. My mom rushed over and, with a giant smile, wrapped her arms around me. She was relieved I was home. I knew she had worried about me the whole time.

I dropped my bags and hugged her back. But no emotion came out. I tried to squeeze her harder and still no love or feeling came out. I tried to stay in the moment with my family but no matter how hard I tried, I couldn't be as joyful to see them as they were to see me. I realized that I left a piece of my mind in Iraq, that something wasn't right. I was supposed to be ecstatic. I was supposed to be full of happiness that my family was reunited with me. I hoped that being at my mom's home for the next couple of days would bring those feelings to the surface.

FLASHBACK

I SPENT THE CAR RIDE BACK TO MY MOM'S HOUSE thinking about life after Iraq. I had seen combat, seen death and destruction, and had experienced every human emotion. The thought of being in society as a combat vet scared me. I didn't know what people would think of me if I told them I fought in the war. I didn't feel I did anything worth sharing that deserved the gratitude of a thank you. I came back home without a kill to show for it.

Society scared me. The very thought of not having a weapon or not knowing the dangers that were out in society made Iraq seem like a walk in the park. I had no idea what to expect. War had a distinct enemy. Your dangers were outlined in detail, in every brief, so that you could recite them word-for-word. You had weapons that could rip the flesh off another individual and trucks built like tanks. You were afraid but you were armed.

Being home in California, there were no convoy briefs, no intelligence reports. The dangers were unknown to me. I had just left one war zone and felt I was coming home to another.

One night at home, I was watching TV, falling in and out of sleep on the living room couch. I heard a loud Boom! Immediately I jumped from the couch, running around the house, looking for my mom. I needed to get her into the garage and stay low so I could set up a defense on the house. A perimeter had to be set, there needed to be grenades setup behind my makeshift fortified barriers.

"Mom, I need you to get into the garage."

My mom stared at me, folding her magazine and setting it down. She didn't bother to move at all, but just gave me a blank stare. I went over to her, to get her moving, but she just sat there, eyes sagging at the corners.

"Mom, we don't have time to waste. I need you to get in the garage. I heard a gunshot."

I needed to find out who was shooting at the house. I didn't want my mom to get hurt or my brother. I ran out of her bedroom looking for my rifle. I knew I had enough ammunition to shoot back. I always brought extra ammunition with me just in case I would use all of it or one of the other guys ran out. But first I had to stay low by the front door in case they started shooting toward the house again. Plus the windows were large so I had to pay special attention to keeping a low profile. I couldn't find my rifle and ran back into my mom's room as I hoped no rounds would ricochet off the walls and kill her.

"Mom, you need to get in the garage now! Someone is shooting at the house."

My mom kept staring at me still with the magazine settled on her lap. I could see there was something bothering her. She had no sense of urgency about rushing to cover. She seemed saddened at the moment but this was no time for emotion, I thought. It was time for us to protect ourselves from being fired at.

But she didn't move. She crossed her hands on her lap, fingers interlaced as her breathing got deeper.

She said, "Michael, there was no gunshot. I didn't hear anything. You're home."

I flipped out thinking how could she not take me serious. This was serious shit. It wasn't a joke. I swear I heard gunshots. Someone was out to get us. I went outside the front door, scanning the entire yard looking for any suspicious activity. I predicted the shooter would move closer toward the house so I had to figure where they were coming from and where I was going to set up to defend the house. I ran inside, pacing around the house, in and out of the different rooms looking for my rifle and items to build cover. My mom came out of her room and walked towards me, to comfort me.

"Michael," she said, "no one is shooting at the house. There is nobody coming after the house or you."

I didn't believe her for a second. I just kept looking for my rifle.

CELEBRATION

THE DRINKING WHEN I CAME BACK STARTED as a celebration of life. I took trips with guys from my unit to Tijuana, Phoenix, everywhere I could to just party and live it up with Jack Daniels and Coke. The trips were liberating times where all we wanted to do was get wasted. The guys I went with were the perfect companions to enjoy our survival.

We embraced each other with a "bro" and "fuck Iraq." Every minute we spent together was when we had booze. Obviously, we never drank at work, considering we would get slammed with every rule in the book if we showed up ready to drive, hammered on Wild Turkey. As soon as our unit released us from work, the drinking started again into the late hours of the night.

Two months being back at Camp Pendleton, the partying started to die down and soon the buddies that surrounded me with bottles were whittled down to just me surrounded with bottles. When I looked for others to drink with me, they were all busy drinking by themselves, too. It was like a huge party in the barracks where everyone came but nobody showed up.

I was honorably discharged from the Marines and still thought I was celebrating life through drinking. My friends back home took me out to bars for weeks enjoying my company. I started college and met some new people but my fear of not being accepted had grown worse with the drinking. I started having a beer or two after school at times. The occasional beer soon turned into a daily beer during the middle of the day. The amount increased to the point where I found myself alone in the middle of the day after class, feeling guilt-ridden because of drinking alone. I knew it didn't feel right but I kept doing it anyway. I was sure that having a one to two beers a day wasn't going to do any harm.

The more I drank, the more I missed the camaraderie of war. Our unit had all been so close and when normal life made its long-awaited appearance, all I wanted was to go back to the Marines to be around my friends. I missed talking stories about the Sandbox and the bond I shared with my friends there. I felt more lost as the months went on. The days after my enlistment ended resulted in paranoia and unparalleled hyper vigilance. Every time a car would backfire, or I heard a loud pop, I went looking for my rifle, scouring my home in the Bay Area for a firearm to protect my family. When I told my mom to get inside the garage and stay low, she didn't laugh at me or point as if to say, "Have you lost your mind?" she just frowned. She knew before I did that my mind had stayed in Iraq and that there was no framework by which I was able to readjust to society. All she could do was sit and watch and continue to be there for me although I never asked her for help. Beer helped somewhat helping my situation a little.

I crossed over into a long period where I showed my fellow students enough kindness and conversation to mask my desire to go back to Iraq and kill. Secretly, Iraq made me feel safe and being at college made me feel that thousands of people would never want to know me.

Every story I told would always be embellished with something new, that I would create in my own mind, because I felt that's what people wanted to hear. It was my own way of gaining acceptance for being in the war. I didn't even bother talk about my real experiences. I didn't bother tell them about the sulfuric smell that made me want to throw up every time I drove by Hit. I hoped that instead of telling them I lived in fear of dying every day and I slept in a barracks room with twenty guys, the details of shooting at little kids and insurgents would make them respect me as a veteran. To me, it wasn't worth it to tell my moments because I thought people wanted to hear the good shit; the stuff they see in movies.

Maybe they would congratulate me, hug me, and this time I would be able to reciprocate that emotion. The thought of celebrating me through my stories made me smile. In a way I was trying to convince myself that war was nothing more than a couple of bumps and bruises by telling stories that showed I had no fear.

THE SANDBOX

Sometimes I didn't even have to say anything. People assumed that because I served in the Marines during war, I must have killed someone. They feared me, too, out of respect for the confirmed kills they assumed I committed. In order for me to feel any acceptance, I usually replied, 'I don't wanna talk about it" to show some sort of trauma from combat. I felt guilt not replying in detail to what really happened but it felt good to be respected.

I portrayed myself as this veteran, alone, surrounded by people who could give a damn about the war and who led their lives in complete ignorance of my service. I viewed my junior college professors as a bunch of pony-tailed hippies who that thought war was the government's ignorant way of obtaining peace instead of talks involving compromise. Even though my experience was first-hand as opposed to what they read in their books during their years in academia, they would shoot my own opinion down in disagreement. To them, the times I did contest their theories on politics and foreign policy they ended up interpreting being defensive about the war in Iraq. It ended up my first couple of semesters not doing well academically. It ended up not going to class during the week. I stopped arguing with them, after a while, choosing to sit at home, crack open a beer, and watch some TV instead of arguing with people that had no idea what war was. Whether it was one drink or a bottle, it made it easier for me not to think or bother to discuss the war with anyone.

WEIGHT

I HAD BEEN OUT OF THE MARINES ABOUT A
year. Autumn was always a great season, where the
leaves were starting to turn dark and the wind was warm
enough to make you feel that summer and fall collided for
the perfect weather. A couple of months into the semes-
ter, my confidence was getting better and I began to make
friends. School was still hard for me, considering I hadn't been
in school for four years and I was more focused on chasing
girls than I was on studying. But it was exciting to start a
new chapter and be around new people.

The walk down to the parking lot on campus was a re-
lief. I was done with classes or on my way to not going to
one. I was starting to thoroughly enjoy transitioning from
the structured military lifestyle into a carefree one, where I
could enjoy the flexibility of the next four years of college.

It was bright and sunny today. No clouds in the sky and
perfect sunglasses weather. I was about to head home and play
some Xbox, drink a beer. My phone rang and I took it out of
my pocket. I saw it was my dad. Usually, when he called, it was
for two reasons. Either he wanted to check in with me, see as

he put it, "If I was still breathing" or he wanted to ask "What's going on with your brother?" As usual, I answered the phone, expecting his usual banter about how Rush Limbaugh despises liberals or how President George W. Bush is a tough guy with a tough job and you should know this since you worked for the President. He paused for a second after my casual "Hello" and said a package from the Marine Corps had come in the mail for me. I was hoping that maybe it was another paycheck, or just another form I had to fill out for my inactive reserve duty.

"Son, you want me to open it?" he said.

"Sure," I said, "it's probably some bullshit form they forgot to give me when I checked out from Camp Pendleton."

I heard the ripping of paper, thinking nothing of it. It could've been anything. But I heard in the news recently that the government was looking to recall some Marines to go back to Iraq for another tour. I didn't think I would get selected, since the odds of me getting selected, having been out of the Marine Corps for only about a year, were really low. There was a pause over the phone. My father was hesitant to speak; I could tell that my father was reading the letter to himself before he could tell me what the letter was. I knew right then that it wasn't just some bullshit form.

"You have been recalled for a pre-screening to deploy for Iraq."

My dad didn't really say much after that. I figured he was waiting for a response from me. I couldn't respond to him though. Immediately when I heard "deploy" and "Iraq" in the same sentence, my mind turned into World War III. All I could think about was violence and terror.

My slow walk down the hill at College of San Mateo turned into a sprint. I ran to my car faster than the times I ran inside from mortar attacks. I needed to figure out what I was supposed to do. How was I supposed to be able to continue to readjust to being home when I was going back to the one place I never wanted to see again? I dropped my phone, feeling a massive amount of anxiety.

The moment I had entered my house, I locked the doors tightly, imitating the countless hours I spent setting up perimeters at Camp Pendleton and simulating a base attack. The floor moved faster underneath my feet as I paced back and forth, counting the steps and processing every scenario as to what I could do to get out of going back to Iraq. What could I do to get out of having to go to that godforsaken hellish place and still be able to return back home normal?

My mother, moments later, walked in the door and I rushed to tell her that I got a letter, and that they could kiss my ass for all I cared. I wasn't going back. I had done two tours. I had driven thousands of miles, dropped off tons of supplies, and survived countless attacks and yet the military felt that wasn't enough.

I cried, tears coming out my eyes, which were full of fear. I told my mom to back the car up over my foot so I couldn't go. At this point, I would do anything to keep me home. She saw that I was not the same; that the war made me into somebody else and that I had lost myself in Iraq. There was a moment where she told me that there was a lot of pain in my eyes. She told me later that day that the fire in my eyes, my passion to make those around me feel like they had known me for years, was gone. She almost grabbed her car keys off the key hooks by the front door so she could run over my foot. But she stopped; that wasn't going to solve anything. She did what any good mother would do; she gave me a hug.

"We will figure it out," she said. "Everything will be okay."

The ongoing battle in my brain affected my state of mind for the next couple of weeks. I stayed at my house a lot, refusing offers to go out to clubs or parties. There was a span of days where I didn't go to school and stayed at my house scared of leaving it. I would have conversations with friends at my and lose track of what was being said. The images of sand and convoys being replayed in my mind kept me from being present.

As much I attempted to deny my mental state and condition, it was too powerful for me to ignore. I tried and tried through every ounce of effort to ignore the horrid images of rounds flying by me, mortars dropping on the ground, and thinking of dying. But no matter what I did to stop the images, I couldn't permanently remove them.

I had no other choice but to go see someone for help since the letter and the images of war were causing me more and more anxiety as each hour passed. I didn't know what was wrong with me, but I knew that since I got the letter from the Marines, my life was in peril. It wasn't normal every five seconds to think of shooting cars to protect the convoy.

THE HOSPITAL

THE VA HOSPITAL SCARED ME. IN PALO ALTO, I was surrounded by older vets who left their cars parked in the lot, walking towards the hospital with the help of their canes, military retired hats worn loosely on their heads. They shook each other's hands in the lobby, waiting to see their doctors as if getting treated here felt more like a social club than it did a hospital. They seemed to enjoy it, probably because they were around other veterans of their time period. Here I was, twenty-four years old and feeling like this was what my future was going to be.

I walked briskly to the doors of the emergency room as they sprung open. It was like they knew everyone that came through those doors needed to be held and cared for.

The triage clerk saw I was lost, and asked in a calm voice, "How can I assist you today?"

"Well, I don't know what's wrong with me but I don't feel like myself."

Without hesitation, she calmly asked if I would sit down. She picked up a red phone, dialing with a sense of urgency, peering through the glass to keep an eye on me. I sat and contemplated my situation. I had taken a huge step after my discharge from the Marines. I was going to school. I was finally feeling like I fit in with everyone else. But now, I was sitting in a chair at the VA hospital, resting the weight of my head in the meaty part of my palms, hoping I wouldn't be locked away in a psych ward.

I was so tired, depressed and feeling now that even if I was doing was the right thing, what would come of this visit? I found myself sitting in this room, tired and emotionally drained, hoping to find out what was wrong with me. I was motivated to move forward in life and put my experiences behind me. I knew it wasn't normal to think of war all the time and it felt every time something great was happening for me, I would have a setback. It felt as if no matter what I did to progress, war was always steps behind me.

Two security guards entered the waiting room and asked me to stand up and follow them. I complied with their request and the triage clerk smiled, reassuring me I was in good hands. The hallways were long, and with every step, the guards walked closer to me, as if I were a convicted felon being escorted to my cell. I was Hannibal Lecter without the face mask. I wasn't going to harm anyone or myself, but the fact these guards, resembling guys who were on the brink of making

NFL teams but got cut on the last day of training camp, were not even two inches away made me feel like I was dangerous.

We arrived at the general physician clinic on the fourth floor, and I was brought to a room where I was seen by three doctors entered in a curious manner. I felt a sense of guilt about taking myself to the hospital to seek help. Since coming home from my first tour, I was warned that seeing a psychiatrist who our unit nicknamed the "Wizard" was a cop-out to avoid redeployment. My command constantly reminded the unit that we signed up for combat and that we must honor our contractual obligations as other Marines had honored theirs. I felt shame in my weakness, especially because I was seeking help from doctors though I hadn't been in the service in over a year.

The three doctors examined every inch of me. I slouched with my feet spread apart as they asked me questions, one after the other. I responded as quickly as I could to each question, but it all made my head spin. I spent hours confessing my most personal thoughts, how I had nightmares about the desert and how I would stare off into the distance while driving on the local highways around my house. I told the doctors the roads made me feel the same terror-filled way when I traveled during convoys to Fallujah and Al Quim.

The feeling of going from combat-proven and patriotic to a specimen didn't sit well with me. I needed help, but I also felt worthless, and it was discomforting having doctors ask me personal questions about combat that I hadn't talked about the whole time I had been home. I just needed to know what was wrong with me, even at the expense of my own self-worth. Maybe this would help me to be able recover some sort of worth in the future.

I spoke in a soft tone, almost as if I had done something horrible. The doctors just nodded in agreement with my answers, like doctors do when they diagnose patients. A few "hmm" and "okays" while scratching notes on their papers was their way of sympathizing with my situation. They soon left, filing out one by one, leaving me in a room filled with silence and cotton swabs. My aggressive, violent, and angry thoughts were so strong that happiness could not deter them. I found myself staring at the wall in front of me, my hands gripping the armrests of the chair as I focused so intently on every medical supply in the room, lost in their details. I was an inanimate object, like those supplies and I took comfort in not moving, breathing just enough to feel my lungs push air in and out while I bonded to the chair under me.

Two of the doctors walked back in and adjusted their thin-frame glasses. One of them just looked down at his notes, addressing me in the same tone that an actor uses in a soap opera when he plays a doctor divulging some deadly illness—the tone they use to kill off actors they want written out of the show. "Mr. Liguori, we have the results of our evaluation in regards to your situation," one of them said. His lab coat was nice and pressed papers sprung out of it, growing upward toward the sky. He just rubbed his index finger and thumb together as he thought about how he was going to tell me what they found. His lip moved to the side, as he calculated the easiest way to explain.

"Yeah and what is it, Doc?"

I had waited patiently for them to reveal their findings. I had answered every question they asked. I told them my stories and every thought implanted against my brain's membrane wall. I gave them everything they needed to make their diagnosis.

"Have you ever heard of PTSD?"

PTSD? Sounded like it was something you caught from a girl you brought home from a bar. I hadn't been with a girl in weeks and now he made me think my skin was going to be green or some shit.

"What the fuck is PTSD?" I replied in a deep, concerned tone, wondering if this was anything incurable.

The doctor paused for a moment as he folded his arms across his chest. He kicked his leg out slightly to prop himself up while he was thinking of how to phrase his diagnosis.

"So, it's called Post Traumatic Stress Disorder and it's an anxiety disorder. Judging by what you have told us and our analysis, we think you have it."

The other stuff he said during his diagnosis I didn't care to listen to. The only things I could focus on were that "anxiety" and "disorder" in the same sentence scared the hell out of me. I left the hospital with nothing but pamphlets about PTSD and a consultation slip to the mental health clinic to see a psychiatrist. There were no security guards escorting me back to my vehicle.

As I left the hospital, I had become a broken man with the weight of war on his broad shoulders. Being given PTSD made me feel that was my societal classification. It made me feel vulnerable, alone, and afraid of what this diagnosis of PTSD had in store for me. I walked out to my car, pamphlets in one hand and slip in the other, looking over both shoulders to check my surroundings.

PAIN

THE NEXT FEW WEEKS WAITING FOR MY appointment with the VA Mental Health Clinic were difficult. I felt myself not speaking in class as much. The realization of my newfound disorder kept me from being social. I had no idea what it was, and the information I researched about PTSD online was not enough to explain my pain. I was afraid that privately entertaining thoughts about killing or leveling small villages that were housing insurgents was becoming better than sex. The love I once had for the Corps and all its traditions was in jeopardy. I served four years honorably and in return, I received PTSD.

I was still conversing with friends, but I never brought up my trip to the hospital or being diagnosed with PTSD. They would not understand, first all, and even if I did tell them, I feared my respect I gained from them would be lost. What were the chances they would know exactly how I felt or what thoughts were in my brain? Being able to tell them about war and the thoughts that go along with was something that truly scared me. I feared acceptance. I feared if I mentioned PTSD, I was to be subjected to judgment. I didn't want to be known as a "crazy war vet."

I visited the mental health clinic weeks later for my appointment. It was quiet inside. Warnings about weapons, self-harm, and overdosing on medications were plastered on the wall in the lobby. It was a welcoming place without the welcome; it kind of made you feel that this is where the abnormal people of society ended up. Guys slouched over in the waiting room, their bellies hanging over the elastic waist banded sweatpants they wore tucked into their combat boots, which they had never taken off since their discharge. This outfit gave them the comfort of civilian life all tucked into the structure of military life. I felt like showing up at the mental health clinic would make me feel that no matter how I dressed or how I acted, my sweats would always be tucked into my boots, too. While I was sitting in that chair in the waiting room, my eyes felt heavy and weighed down, as if hooks were dragging them to the ground. I couldn't grasp that I was actually in the clinic getting help; that my mental burden was possibly going to be managed through meds and everlasting countless sessions that would last a lifetime. That's the last thing I wanted, to ask for help but I caved into the idea that I needed it, whether with meds or with therapy. I needed something to get me through each day of living. Maybe it would've been both. I would never know though, without seeing a psychiatrist.

My name was called and I was escorted by a pony-tailed, hippie doctor who was short with me, communicating in short sentences like "How are you?" and, "Did the nurse talk to you?" His room was typical of a doctor's office, a couple of chairs slightly separated to signify the extent of the patient-doctor closeness. A certificate of his Ph.D. hung in the middle of the otherwise empty wall. The conversation started with, "So, tell me why you're here." It seems pretty obvious why I was here, so I responded for what felt like the millionth time that "I have PTSD and I need to seek treatment options." I've had so many doctors and family ask me about PTSD in the preceding weeks that I should've made handouts or a PowerPoint presentation.While I sat there pouring my heart out to this doctor, all his responses were just like the doctors I met at the hospital weeks prior: stone-faced and disconnected. He didn't look at me once, as I focused on him, attempting to establish some sort of human connection. He jotted and scribbled notes all over his yellow pad. He wrote short sentences, and nodded his head as if confirm that his conclusions correlated with what I had said. He squinted his eyes, pressing hard on the paper with his pen while the tendons in his skinny hand strained and popped out.

I thought my venting about war in this one session with him would be all the therapy I needed. I needed just one good vent session, where a medical professional could just listen to what I wanted and needed to say. To be honest, I felt the best way for me to start treatment was by just talking to someone. That was my own personal diagnosis.

He finished his notes, interrupting me as I was about to tell him one of the many incidents that I couldn't get out of my head.

"So, I know it's a difficult time for you and everything. I'm going to recommend some anti-depressants and therapy which will allow you to work through your struggles."

Anti-what? I didn't want those things. I just wanted to talk to someone. But I hadn't been myself since deployment and everything that happened in the recent weeks made me open to any suggestion for treatment.

At the end of the session, he told me to take the prescription that I held in my loosened grip and bring it to the pharmacy counter when I left his office. I gave him an insincere "thank you," smiling as big as I could in the hopes that he wouldn't see that I didn't feel comfortable accepting his recommendation. But he was a doctor and he had experienced in dealing with guys like me.

I just kept looking at the paper with his chicken scratch on it, wondering if I was doing the right thing for myself. I had never been on meds, or "happy pills," before, and here I was caving into this idea that they would make all my worries and troubles disappear. I was scarred by that place and I knew that my thoughts, without any treatment, could become worse than they were. I was so desperate to get help and have PTSD go away that anything he would've said to me that day, I would've done, even if it meant brain surgery.

The pharmacy was painted the same color as the walls, an earthy tone with small scuff marks spread throughout. At the window, I handed my prescription to the clerk and moments later received a bottle, filled to the brim, with my name all in caps. It was slid underneath the counter window with what seemed like a sense of urgency, like she was trying to get me the pills as fast as she could so I could take them. I looked at it, hoping that they were going to allow me to feel happiness and normalcy. I thought, maybe the doctor was right about his recommendation. A good dose of these daily may make me feel will kind of how I use to be before the war.

The pills worked well for the first week. I was able to continue my studies and have conversations with girls and my friends without having to discuss Iraq. My attention span increased in conversation and I felt more interactive with others. I felt accepted. Weeks went on and I continued to take them, even though it didn't feel right that I was taking pills to make myself happy. It didn't make me feel comfortable but at least the thoughts were going away.

My face started to hurt from smiling so much. The pain in my cheeks I knew would go away eventually but I still felt a sense of guilt seeking pills for a false sense of happiness. I was high on serotonin all day and by the time I came home I was exhausted enough that I couldn't strike up a conversation with anyone. But when my family would start to talk to me, I responded. The fatigue eventually took over but the fact I was able to give them any sort of answer to how my day was felt like progress. The pain in my cheeks, the bags under my eyes, the responses, this was all worth it I thought. It felt good to be "normal."

BOB

AFTER A COUPLE OF MONTHS OF TAKING pills, I decided one day to stop taking them. The guilt each time I took one became stronger and stronger, and eventually I caved in to my own pressure. I didn't know at the time that when taking any antidepressant or any medication, you needed to wean yourself off of them slowly. I had stopped taking them "cold turkey" and found the thoughts about war and killing grew increasingly strong in my brain.

After my grades had progressed to higher marks, they dropped again due to my excess absences from class and depressive states. I felt more depressed, more anxious around others, particularly in large crowds more often. The guilt from taking pills subsided but now I found myself, with no help and no therapy, on the brink of self-destruction. It felt that despite getting off the pills, I was now in a state of instability that brought me down to a lower level in life

I didn't feel comfortable going back to the VA. I didn't want to be put back on more medication so I ended up seeing a counselor that my father recommended to me. He felt that maybe talking to someone on the outside would work best for me since the counselor wasn't a licensed psychiatrist. My father had problems and had reached a point in his life where his spirituality was unknown to him. I felt maybe that part of the reason I was feeling more depressed and more anxious besides the pills was I had no connection to anything spiritual or a higher power.

My father was a firm believer in God and figured that my loss of faith overseas happened because of the war. He thought renewing my faith would heal me and give me some guidance to my everyday anxiety. My father told me that God will always be there and that "eventually son, you will have to face him someday when you go to see him upstairs." He made it sound like I was running from the law and eventually I was going to have to turn myself in.

His personal experience with God didn't touch me as I thought it did but rather encouraged me to find myself as a young adult. He made mistakes as a young man, did some things against his better judgment that he never should've done. When I was about ten years old, he told me God appeared to him. Since then, my father was all about God and Jesus, figuring the past years, when he walked down the path of broken souls, could be fixed with his newly restored faith.

But my dad never questioned his own existence on a daily basis after serving in combat. He didn't know what it was like to see hatred, have mortars drop in on you, and be scared for your life. I was just hoping that talking to his counselor would help me believe in something.

His name was Bob. He was always welcoming when I went to see him. The first time we met, he had the most calming demeanor I have ever encountered. He was soft-spoken, dressed a lot like Ned Flanders from *The Simpsons* (except without the glasses) and would say he "saw God's good in everything." He always sat down after me and semi-crossed his legs when we talked, forming a right triangle with his lower half.

During our initial session, I told Bob my stories about war and how I was taking pills until almost a week ago. As I was continuing to explain my thoughts, Bob interrupted me and asked a question with the utmost curiosity.

"Do you feel God exists, Michael?"

It was the first time, out of any of the therapists I had seen, that any one of them asked me a question about religion. It caught me off guard. My feelings about God came and went and recently, I put the whole religious situation on the back burner. I didn't feel that PTSD and war had anything to do with whether or not God is real.

Since I had seen war, I slowly forced God slowly out of my life, forced out by the mortars and kids throwing grenades. I struggled with the conundrum of how does an all-powerful being like God put me through all of this? Why would he let me feel anger without ever feeling happy? War was the only thing that was tangible to me. It was the only thing I knew existed. I didn't know if God truly existed anymore after my combat tours.

But I couldn't say all of that to him. I didn't want him to look down upon me. I paused, rubbing my hands together as I responded the only way I knew how to.

"I don't know."

During future sessions, I explained my stories to the fullest detail, every turn of every road I traveled on. Somehow, Bob was under the impression that I wasn't here to talk about the war. But it was all I could talk about with him. I didn't know how to talk about spirituality or religion when I didn't know what I believed in.

His question of if I believed in God's existence came up so much during all of our sessions that I gave in and discussed the whole God question. I cried in those sessions when it came to my beliefs. Every time I did, I did what every man attempts to do to conceal their vulnerability. I'd say stupid or corny like "Something is in my eye" or "I'm not crying. The dry air is making my eyes water." You know, some response.

Once the tears started to flow, I pulled tight on the reins, only allowing a drop to crawl down the side of my face. Then I would slowly put my feelings back in their box and lock them up. I had one last session with Bob before I was to head out to Missouri and check in for pre-screening. He wrote a letter at my request, to help supplement the findings of the VA doctors, and to give the Marines more evidence for me not to go back. After he wrote the letter during our session, he quietly looked at me in the eyes, putting his hand on my shoulder, saying,

"No matter what happens, God is with you."

He gave me a slight pat on the back and a look of confidence that God would find his way back into my heart. I just looked at him, attempting to hold back the tears, not wanting to assure him that he was right. I admittedly did not want to accept he was. I left his office, with my note in hand, hoping that this was enough, along with my medical records, to get me back to California to start a new chapter in my life after closing the book on the Marines.

At times, I think about how much Bob did for me. He was able to see through my hardened exterior and see how torn up I was. Bob never forced God on me but simply wanted me to consider finding him again. He figured talking to me about what I believe in would give me some stability to my situation. He wanted me to see that having faith can go a long way. If I was able to wrap my head around the idea that having faith would put my anxiety at ease, life at home despite my experiences would allow me to be myself again. Bob explained God would bear everything I had suffered on his shoulders.

BUS

I GOT TO MISSOURI AND TOUCHED DOWN IN Kansas City. A bunch of guys were shaking their heads in disbelief that they were being recalled, like me. Many of them were guys I had served with; even some guys from my platoon. It was one of the most interesting things to see guys transformed from strictly regulated Marines to long-haired, bearded, burly men who were either digging gold in the mountains of Alaska, or driving freight liners, all while they attempted to pursue their bachelor's degrees. Some of them you could tell were plagued by problems when they were home. They started drinking right before the bus pulled up, bags under their eyes, fear and whiskey etched deeply on their faces and on their breath. They also felt the same way I did; there was no reason for us to be here after we already gave ourselves unselfishly to America.

The bus pulled up and we filed in one-by-one. Immediately the bus ride over to the air force base on the outskirts of the city became a comedy show. Comments about smoking dope and taking a shitload of drugs before they saw the doctors were followed by laughter and remarks. There were even some guys who mentioned they were at a rave for three days banging lines of cocaine into their heads and partying recklessly, since they knew that they had nothing to hold them back from getting reactivated. Some guys even said they would jump off the roof at this base, hoping to break their legs just so they wouldn't have to go.

One of the guys, named Bismarck, talked about how he wanted to get out of redeploying. "Man, I'll tell you right now. If I had the damn chance when I thought about it, I should've been drunk as fuck and had my dad roll over my foot with the truck. My ass would never be going back."

Guys were shaking their heads in agreement. None of us wanted to go back and the more stories I heard about ways to get out of this recall, the more tempted I was to even bang some lines of cocaine to my own head, even if it meant being messed up for the next couple of days.

A kid who was on the outside of the inner circle we had created in the back didn't really say anything until he heard of the guy's plans. He gently turned around from his front seat just at the right time, and walked over to our group when the laughter died down.

"See, your plan would be great, but here's the deal. I had a friend who got recalled and his buddy who was with him did the same shit you were talking about. Talking about how he wanted to break his foot and be on all these drugs so he didn't have to go back. Truth is, the guy broke his foot, smoked some pot before he came here, and was thinking the whole time that he was going to get out of it. Never happened. The Government don't care, man. They don't give a shit about us at all. To them, we are numbers. Some of ya'll seem to forget what kind of number you are. You are nothing but a Social Security Number. It will never change. Just like this guy, it will never change. He never got denied. They just waited for his foot to heal and since he popped on his drug test, they filed charges against him because he still was under contract. And he still had to go back to the Middle East."

The kid had made the bus ride turn somber. After we had laughed for so long, joking about ways to get out, he had put a reality check on the situation. It was true. We were just numbers to them. They knew nothing about our interests, thoughts, or even passions in life. The silence blanketed the bus for the remainder of the trip, turning the comedy show into awkward whispered conversations. We were the last four of our Social Security Number and that's all we could ever be.

I ended being disqualified for deployment due to having PTSD. They deemed that I was too much of a liability and giving me a gun would not be a wise decision because of my diagnosis. I was extremely happy that I wasn't going back to Iraq. I called my family who were excited to hear the news. My friends, crying with joy, were thankful. Little did I know that the struggle with PTSD had begun.

KITCHEN

YEARS LATER, I FELT MYSELF starting to feel normal again. I ended up reconnecting with old friends, working a couple jobs, and played college football. But the war in my mind was still there. All those things helped but the war never left. It hindered my ability to be normal. The more I told it to leave my mind, it came back stronger. It drove me mad.

THE SANDBOX

I decided to try counseling again at the VA with the encouragement of my girlfriend hoping that this time around, I wouldn't be given pills. I could just talk to a doctor without any medications. The sessions were some of the hardest things I ever had done. I talked for 90 minutes each time, working through each scenario, each thought I had wondering what the reason was behind my trauma. I felt I made great progress, gaining some perspective on the war in my head. But being intense therapy also brought me to a moment that changed my life forever.

There was one time, where my thoughts were so strong and overpowering, the pain was so great, I thought about wanting to end my life. I felt that no matter what I did, the thoughts of war, depression, and fear would never go away. I walked upstairs into my kitchen, convincing myself with each step that I was going to go through with it. It seemed like the only answer.

Slowly, I walked to the knife drawer and opened it. I gazed at each knife blade as it lay next to the other. I looked at how sharp they were and thought that the quicker I went through with ending my life, the faster I would be free from my emotional burden. I didn't care about anything else or what was to come of me after my death. All I cared about was that the thoughts would go away. It was the only thing I could think of doing. All the medications, therapy, crying randomly it would all stop. I would be somewhere else without suffering.

As soon as I was close to executing this plan, my house became very quiet. I felt a light coat, a comforting pair of hands wrap around me. I was scared, petrified, as my hand couldn't move toward the blade. My mind became clear, with no more thoughts of harming myself or of war. I no longer feared my existence or felt any pain.

A voice in my right ear, soothing and compassionate, spoke to me. It was a deep voice full of serenity. I looked my hand, still scared out of my mind, not knowing if it was my subconscious that was speaking to me or whoever it was. My hand still could not move toward the blade. I felt the hairs on my arm stand up, my eyes closed. The voice said things to me in the most calming manner as I felt the most pure, tranquil moment of my life.

"Michael, put the knife down, son. It is not your time to go."

The voice was so caring and compassionate that I felt as if I had been injected in my arms with unconditional love. I paused for a breath as I filled with emotion. My whole life since I came home from Iraq had no purpose. I felt I was this monster, this machine that would never be able to know anything else except war. I felt lost, unsure of what was out there for me in life, and who God really was. I never knew that at my darkest moment when I felt my own world collapsing on top of me, God who I had pushed away after all the times I saw violence, would save my life.

I closed the drawer after the voice spoke to me, slamming it shut as I cried the hardest I have ever cried. I let everything pour out of me. The bottled-up thoughts, the fears, everything came out in a torrential downpour of tears. I couldn't go through with killing myself and putting my family and my friends through hell. I turned around and walked downstairs. The whole rest of the day I sat on my couch thinking of what just happened and what was I to do now. All I knew at that moment was that God had saved me from myself.

Afterword

SERVING IN COMBAT IS A RITE OF PASSAGE
for a Marine. To be able to holster your rifle, magazine inserted with a round loaded in the chamber, and fire
it at an enemy gives you credibility as combat-hardened
man. The moment I signed the papers to join, I knew that
combat was in my future. It was what I wanted. Even the
recruiter asked if I thought that I would end up going to
Iraq. I nodded my head at him as sure as ever. After what
happened with the two planes crashing into the World Trade
Center on 9/11, I was so enraged that I would've left the
day after if I weren't still in high school. I love my country
and the belief that every person has the right to live free.

When I was 18 years old, the Marines seemed so simple.
"Give us the next four years of your life and we will take
care of you." I wanted to serve my country and the deal
the recruiter offered me was too good to pass up. I'd have a
place to stay, money for college, and even training on how
to fight were these things I could only dream of. But what
I got most out of the Marines wasn't any of those things
that were offered to me that day. I did get a place to stay.
The Marines paid for my school. The training in mixed

martial arts was great. What I got the most was a lifetime of stories and friends that turned into my second family.

The stories I have written are accounts of what happened in my unit during Operation Iraqi Freedom Part II and III in Al Asad and Al-Taquddum, Iraq. I was part of a motor transportation unit tasked with resupplying all the Forward Operating Bases in the Al-Anbar province. These stories are all things that bring me tears of joy and sadness. There are days that I wake up and all I think about is the times out in Iraq. I think about my friends that I was with during the long convoys through desert roads filled with danger, the conversations I had in the barracks late night on duty, and how lucky I am to be alive.

Yet, with all these stories and my newfound outlook on life, I also had to write about the dark side of war and the journey that got me here. I had to write about home, about fear and my hidden battle I fight every day of my life. It's the same battle that many men and women who served in combat come home and face in their own lives.

Post-Traumatic Stress Disorder (PTSD) can ruin your life. It can keep you from being human. All you ever think about is the trauma. The night terrors and limited amount of sleep take a toll on your body. I was diagnosed a year after being discharged from the Marines and it brought me to rock bottom. It ruined my relationships, my friendships, and my life. There are days where I wish I never had it. I wish I never had to experience what I did because it has been etched in my brain for eternity. After the completion of this book, I realized that despite all my regrets of having it, the war in Iraq and the daily fight with PTSD make me stronger every day.

I have been to the depths of my own hell. I have seen what life is like when isolation and alcohol are your only friends. But I also have seen what it is like to receive love again. I have an amazing group of people who never turned their backs on me.

When it felt so easy to quit living, they never gave up on me, never doubted my abilities. When I thought all was lost, they were by my side with open arms. Today, because of the support I have received, I am able to tell my story. I am able to talk about the trials of my life and share it with all of you. I am grateful and truly humble that you would take time to read this book.

America's war on PTSD is better but not where it could be. There is still a lot more to be done. The layers of combat tours piled one upon another still are damaging to generations of veterans. We cannot go back in time and make things different for them. We cannot change the outcome of any war experience they had. What we can change is the future for our veterans.

After I finished writing *The Sandbox*, I created a non-profit named Operation Work Warriors that provides educational career assistance to combat and military veterans. My intent is to make the transition home easier for future veterans than my journey reintegrating into society. I want to make them feel they can come home and achieve more. Surviving war is a great achievement in itself but I hope that veterans will see that our country needs us in the workforce to start new companies. Society needs veterans in the community to be leaders, make positive changes in the world.

Thank you for reading this book. I hope you enjoy it as much as I did writing it.